OBSESSION
AND
RELEASE

OBSESSION
AND
RELEASE
Rereading the Poetry
of Louise Bogan

Lee Upton

Lewisburg
Bucknell University Press
London: Associated University Presses

Associated University Presses
440 Forsgate Drive
Cranbury, NJ 08512

Associated University Presses
16 Barter Street
London WC1A 2AH, England

Associated University Presses
P.O. Box 338, Port Credit
Mississauga, Ontario
Canada L5G 4L8

The paper used in this publication meets the requirements of the American National Standard for Permanence of Paper for Printed Library Materials Z39.48-1948.

Library of Congress Cataloging-in-Publication Data

Upton, Lee, 1953–
    Obsession and release : rereading the poetry of Louise Bogan / Lee Upton.
        p.   cm.
    Includes bibliographical references and index.
    ISBN 0-8387-5321-3 (alk. paper)
    1. Bogan, Louise, 1897–1970—Criticism and interpretation.
2. Women and literature—United States—History—20th century.
3. Repression (Psychology) in literature. 4. Subconsciousness in literature. I. Title.
PS3503.0195Z89   1996
811'.52—dc20   96-2101
                                                                         CIP

PRINTED IN THE UNITED STATES OF AMERICA

Contents

Acknowledgments

I am grateful to Ruth Limmer, the literary executor of Louise Bogan's estate, who has allowed me to quote from Bogan's poems, essays, letters, journals, and other materials. I am indebted as well to Tanya Solomon at Farrar, Straus & Giroux, Inc., who aided me in attaining permissions for use of poems from *The Blue Estuaries*.

Jeredith Merrin provided invaluable advice as a knowledgeable and perceptive reader of the manuscript, and I am deeply thankful for her richly detailed comments. Mills F. Edgerton Jr. deserves my thanks for bringing my manuscript to her attention.

My debt extends to the editors who first published my articles on Louise Bogan. R. K. Meiners at the *Centennial Review* published "The Re-Making of a Poet: Louise Bogan" in 1992, and Charlotte Walker and Kathleen O'Mara of *Phoebe: An Interdisciplinary Journal of Feminist Scholarship, Theory and Aesthetics* published "Violent Practices: The Poetry of Louise Bogan" in 1990.

Patricia A. Donahue was unfailingly encouraging, and Bin Ramke was supportive in our discussions from the very beginning of this project.

Without any special pleading on my part, Paul Schlueter and James Woolley found books by Bogan that were out of print and generously made them available to me.

The librarians at Lafayette College have been very helpful. I am especially grateful to Betsy Moore, Janemarie Berry, and Richard Everett. I am also thankful for the assistance of John Lancaster, curator of Special Collections at the Amherst Library, where the Louise Bogan Papers are housed.

I thank the members of the Committee on Academic Research at Lafayette College for their support.

Jill Riefenstahl provided excellent (and good-humored) secretarial assistance.

Michael Koy, Christine Retz, and Evelyn Apgar shepherded my manuscript through the publication process with absolute professionalism.

I thank Wyatt Benner for his scrupulous care in copyediting my manuscript. This book is stronger for his attention.

My greatest debt is to Eric J. Ziolkowski who read this study several times, offering thoughtful and plentiful advice and kind encouragement at every stage of the process. I thank our daughter, Theodora, whose birth coincided with—and further enlivened—my early researches on Bogan.

Eleanore Novello entered my family's life during the early stages of my writing of this book. Her exceptional spirit affected us all deeply. This book is dedicated to her memory.

Grateful acknowledgment is made to individuals and publishers who gave permission to reprint copyrighted material:

The Blue Estuaries: Poems 1923–1968, by Louise Bogan. © 1968 by Louise Bogan. Excerpts reprinted by permission of Farrar, Straus & Giroux, Inc. and Ruth Limmer, literary executor of Louise Bogan's estate.

Body of This Death, by Louise Bogan. © 1923 by Robert M. McBride & Company; © 1996 by Ruth Limmer. Excerpts reprinted by permission of Ruth Limmer.

Journey Around My Room: The Autobiography of Louise Bogan, A Mosaic, edited and assembled by Ruth Limmer; © 1980 by Ruth Limmer. Excerpts reprinted by permission of Ruth Limmer.

A Poet's Alphabet: Reflections on the Literary Art and Vocation, edited by Robert Phelps and Ruth Limmer. New York: McGraw-Hill. © 1970. Excerpts reprinted by permission of Ruth Limmer.

What the Woman Lived: Selected Letters of Louise Bogan, 1920–1970, edited by Ruth Limmer. New York: Harcourt Brace Jovanovich. © 1973. Excerpts reprinted by permission of Ruth Limmer.

"Art Embroidery," © 1928, by the *New Republic.* Excerpts reprinted by permission.

"Hidden," © 1936 by the *New Yorker,* reprinted by permission.

"Poetesses in the Parlor," © 1936 by the *New Yorker.* Excerpts reprinted by permission.

"The Springs of Poetry," © 1923, by the *New Republic.* Excerpts reprinted by permission.

"Virginia Woolf on Women," © 1929, by the *New Republic.* Excerpts reprinted by permission.

Material in the Louise Bogan Papers, Special Collections Department, Amherst College Library, is reprinted by permission of the Trustees of Amherst College and Ruth Limmer, © 1996.

"Violent Practices: The Poetry of Louise Bogan," by Lee Upton, appeared in *Phoebe: An Interdisciplinary Journal of Feminist Scholarship, Theory and Aesthetics* 2, no. 2 (1990). Excerpts reprinted by permission.

"The Re-Making of a Poet: Louise Bogan," by Lee Upton, appeared in *Centennial Review* 36, no. 3 (1992). Reprinted by permission.

Abbreviations

BTD   *Body of This Death*. New York: Robert M. McBride, 1923.

BE   *The Blue Estuaries: Poems, 1923–1968*. New York: Ecco, 1977.

JAR   *Journey Around My Room: The Autobiography of Louise Bogan, a Mosaic*. Edited by Ruth Limmer. New York: Viking, 1980.

OBSESSION
AND
RELEASE

Introduction

Rather than a repressed poet as she is figured in much contemporary criticism, Louise Bogan may be more accurately viewed as a poet self-consciously studying repression in poems of extreme confrontation, reflecting an aesthetic of rupture and difference, and in complex ways intimating the workings of the unconscious. Repeatedly, Bogan based her authority as a poet on her allegiance to the subversive unconscious rather than on cultural law.

That Bogan remains absent or nearly so from many contemporary discussions of modern poetry may mean that readers have not risen to the peculiar challenges of her poetry and that, as Martha Collins suggests, we must freshly attempt to understand the "pleasure" that this poetry arouses.[1] Of course reputation, a fitful wind, may often change direction for a poet. After a poet's death, reputation may shift even more wildly, for whether poets are born or made, surely they are remade by their critics. Bogan's critical reception is a curious case in point.

In much early criticism, Bogan is considered as an exception among women. Allen Tate's discussion serves as an example: "Women, I suppose, are fastidious, but many women poets are fastidious in their verse only as a way of being finical about themselves. But Miss Bogan is a craftsman in the masculine mode."[2] In his review of *Dark Summer*, Louis Untermeyer argues that the book's "quality lifts it high above the merely adequate writing published in such quantities by women in these so literate states."[3] In the most often cited account of Bogan's poetry, Theodore Roethke similarly chooses to make Bogan an exception to her sex. In a catalog that has since achieved notoriety, he decries those female poets engaged in "lamenting the lot of the woman; caterwauling; writing the same poem about fifty times, and so on," but argues that "Louise Bogan is something else."[4] What that "something else" might be has puzzled critics before and since.

15

In more recent critical reconstructions, Bogan appears problematic for reasons that, paradoxically, prove similar to those which Tate, Untermeyer, and Roethke project. In the more recent remaking of the poet, Bogan again serves as an exception of sorts—an isolated and gifted poet, yet one removed from healthy self-affirmation, excluded not only by patriarchy but circumscribed, as Gloria Bowles in particular contends, by her own internalization of male modernism's disdain for women's poetry and "'female emotion.'"[5] As Gwendolyn Sorell Sell has protested, often current criticism makes Bogan into "a patriarchal cripple."[6] She is seen as a victim identified with her oppressors, narrowly focused in theme, devoted to a male structure of values and yet confined within the lyric as women's traditional province.

In different mixtures, much recent criticism reconfigures Bogan by three principal means. First, critics construe her work through metaphors of ingestion, often in terms of a suspect growth, the cancer of an internalized male value system that consumes her scope and accomplishment. Second, critics express repulsion from Bogan's autobiographical reticence, a reticence that counters a strain within Anglo-American feminist criticism that prizes rhetorical directness and autobiographical revelation. And, finally, critics place her work in an evolutionary frame, judging Bogan to be a stern and repressed ancestor from whom contemporary women poets must diverge in style and viewpoint.

The construction of Bogan's poetry in the light of self-consumption may be especially revealing. Deborah Pope describes Bogan's poetry written after her first book, *Body of This Death* (1923), as "distrustful, cynical . . . built on a reduction of the human and natural landscape."[7] Bogan's work is cited as "a poetry of no return"[8] in which the poet makes "femaleness itself . . . a constitutional flaw."[9] Bogan is viewed as distanced from her actual body and victimized by an alien value structure that she has internalized. As a consequence, Bogan and her poetry would seem to have little "body" left: "Tragically, what seems least to fit [in this poetry] is the female body itself."[10] In somewhat similar terms, Patrick Moore begins his essay by remarking that "Styles are symptoms," and finds much of Bogan's poetry to be "a wasteland of anxiety and repression," where "true feelings are blurred by symbol, distanced by masks, muted by form." Hers is a style, he observes, that is "rare, if not impossible, in a feminist poet."[11] Dominating such symptoms is a dubious "maleness," a value structure that dismisses women's achievements and constrains Bogan to a suspect goal of formal perfection. Bowles maintains that Bogan's poetry "is an extreme example of a woman's internalization of male ideas of the woman poet."[12] In her turn, Mary K. DeShazer, despite her revisionary account of the poet's employment of silence, similarly finds her subject to be hampered by "a male-defined concept of the woman artist."[13] And Kate Daniels defines Bogan, whom she links with Sylvia Plath, as "undeniably self-destructive" and possessed of "antifeminist impulses."[14]

A word frequently heard in some estimates is "limitation." Bogan's body of just over a hundred poems, her conception of the woman poet's role, and her refusal of self-disclosure are cited as limiting factors. Over fifty years ago Allen Tate depicted Bogan as a poet who practices "a strict observance of certain limitations."[15] Yvor Winters described her "subject-matter, or rather attitude" as "central, as fundamental, as any attitude so limited could be."[16] On a less ambiguous note, Llewellyn Jones argued that Bogan's poetry is poised "against the limitations, imposed and self-imposed, on women; and at the same time [it creates] a cry for something positive, for something compelling."[17] Léonie Adams observed that Bogan's poetry remains "an art of limits, the limit of the inner occasion and of the recognized mode."[18] More recently, Bowles titled her 1987 study *Louise Bogan's Aesthetic of Limitation*, defining this poet's working practice as "a strict idea of what a woman poet could and could not permit herself."[19] Echoing Bowles in 1992, Elizabeth Dodd frames Bogan's "reticence" as "sometimes . . . a kind of artistic repression," and thus a form of limitation.[20]

Antagonism toward Bogan's insistence on privacy further focuses criticism. Her omissions of direct autobiographical details strike critics as repressive. Bowles, for instance, argues that Bogan's "compacted forms, her suppressions and obscurities, are her declaration of the near impossibility—even in the twentieth century—of being both woman and poet."[21] Suzanne Clark, who has written one of the most compelling recent chapters focusing on Bogan, reveals in her conclusion her own mixed feelings about the poet's style in a manner that at least in part supports Bowles's: "The intensity, the condensation, the overdetermination of [Bogan's] poems keep the alarming news [of her poetry] confined and may even allow the resistant reader to leave them behind as beautiful objects."[22] In more dire terms, Pope maintains that Bogan's poems reflect "the exclusion and suppression of any nature and life that does not fit her frame," declaring that Bogan developed "a style and stance pared to the bone: the granite hill that is both imprisoning and terrible."[23] In Pope's study Bogan is reduced to a variation of the critic's theme of isolation. Representing victimhood, her work is characterized by "powerlessness and extreme bitterness," "alienation from the body," and "a posture of renunciation."[24] Sandra M. Gilbert and Susan Gubar, drawing on Bowles and a brief portion of Bogan's correspondence, consign her situation to that of a "paradigm." As such, Bogan is made rhetorically effective, a trope for women's historical oppression and "self-loathing."[25] Implicitly, Bogan becomes a disempowered figure: a stunted ancestor whose alleged failures serve as a point of departure for theory.

In another brief discussion that presents Bogan emblematically, Paula Bennett follows an evolutionary rubric. Bennett examines in women's poetry the emergence of Medusa, the mythological figure upon whom one of Bogan's central poems focuses. Bennett argues that women validate through Medusa "those aspects of their being that their families and society have invalidated by treating such qualities as unfeminine and unacceptable."[26] Recast in contemporary poetry, Medusa becomes Bennett's symbol of the woman poet's self-empowerment. Nevertheless, such a self is seen as beyond the focal experience of Louise Bogan. Bogan's "Medusa," the earliest poem that Bennett draws upon, emerges in her analysis as devoid of "life" and "tragically appropriate for a poet of extraordinary gifts who believed only 105 of her poems worthy of permanent record and who appears to have despised the very idea that she might be considered a woman poet."[27] In Bennett's brief discussion, Bogan becomes a psychological victim of the Gorgon's paralysis. Lauding a contemporary poet for a poem on Medusa that "hurts to read" and reveals "ugliness," Bennett casts Bogan in contrast as a petrified specimen of repression. In Bennett's and other such analyses, Bogan emerges as a bad patient of sorts, refusing the medicine of acceptance and seemingly neglectful of what Bennett calls in another context "the true self within."[28] In such discussions, particularly in those of Pope and Bennett, a strange split figure arises, for lingering behind them is a ghost image of a projected Louise Bogan: a healed and generous figure, a foremother whose "true self within" might emerge at last.

Through a number of recent reconstructions, Bogan assumes the position of a limited (and limiting) predecessor to the contemporary poet. She is perceived as internalizing "maleness," circumscribing her emotional range, and depicting female victims without imagining a more positive conception of women. Unhappily, such analyses of Bogan's poetry often fail to contend fully with the fruitfully disturbing subjects of stasis and rupture, gender impositions, and release (the latter, most clearly within her last poems, laboriously wrested from silence) that pervade her poetry.

Although Bogan has been criticized as a poet of "suppressions"—that is, of omitting references to her life circumstances to the detriment of her work—Bogan was little given to writing poetry that did not deal in some way with her experience. Lyric poetry, she believed, grew from emotion that was based on experience. In a letter of 1966 she observed: "It is difficult to analyze lyric poetry, because, if it is at all authentic, it is based on emotion—on some actual occasion, some real confrontation."[29] Indeed, what Bogan presents is experience as it has been cast into patterns that allow unconscious energies to saturate the poem. As a consequence, in readings of her poetry I have at times turned to her autobiographical writings, for her poetry seems to "absorb" or "translate" the deepest elements of her experience.

In her prose piece "Journey Around My Room," Bogan contemplates beginnings in a manner that addresses her own origins: *"The initial mystery that attends any journey is: how did the traveller reach his starting point in the first place?"* (*JAR* 2). Bogan's lower-middle-class beginnings as the daughter of a mill-town foreman subject to frequent relocations mark her poems and prose; she did not forget her entry on the periphery of a more stable social world. Born 11 August 1897 in Livermore Falls, Maine, Bogan was the second child and only daughter of Mary (Murphy) Shields and Daniel J. Bogan. She recalls that her own journey began with violence. "I must have experienced violence from birth," she wrote in her journal (*JAR* 24). Her poems register the disorder of a childhood marred by fierce quarrels between her parents and the effects of her mother's extramarital affairs and recurrent, mysterious absences from home. In some measure, Bogan's preoccupation with betrayal emerges from her earliest experiences, especially those involving her mother. "I cannot describe or particularize," she wrote in a journal entry. "Surely all this agony has long since been absorbed into my work. Even then, it was beginning to be absorbed. For I began writing—at length, in prose—in 1909 . . . I began to write verse from about fourteen on. The life-saving process then began. By the age of 18 I had a thick pile of manuscript, in a drawer in the dining room—and had learned every essential of my trade" (*JAR* 50).

She was educated in classical literature at the Girls' Latin School in Boston, and in 1915 received one year of education at Boston University. In 1916 she married a soldier, German-born Curt Alexander, and in May of the following year, four months pregnant, she joined him in the Panama Canal Zone. In October she gave birth to her only child, Mathilde (Maidie) Alexander. In the following year she would separate from her husband, with whom she shared few interests, returning to Boston with her daughter. During the same year her brother Charles, a soldier in World War I, was killed in action in France, and Bogan temporarily reunited with her husband. The couple separated in 1919, and in the following year her husband died of pneumonia.

In telling terms, Bogan characterized her youth to her friend, the critic Morton D. Zabel:

I never was a member of a "lost generation." I was the highly charged
and neurotically inclined product of an extraordinary childhood and an un-
fortunate early marriage, into which last state I had rushed to escape the
first. *** I had no relations whatever with the world about me; I lived in a
dream, populated by figures out of Maeterlinck and Pater and Arthur Symons
and Compton Mackenzie (*Sinister Street* and *Sylvia Scarlett* made a great
impression on me) and H. G. Wells and Francis Thompson and Alice Meynell
and Swinburne and John Masefield and other oddly assorted authors. What I
did and what I felt was, I assure you, *sui generis.*[30]

After her husband's death, Bogan lived in New York City on her widow's
pension, leaving her daughter to be raised during weekdays by her parents.
She worked in branches of the New York Public Library and Brentano's
Bookstore, and in 1922 she lived in Vienna for six months, studying piano,
reading, and writing poems. She had already published poems in *Others* in
1917, and in 1921 five of her poems were accepted for publication in *Poetry*.
     Bogan's commitment to lyric poetry was fully forged by this time. She
had few doubts, it would seem, of her possession of the essential for the
lyric poet, the "lyric gift": "The practice of lyric poetry—the most intense,
the most condensed, the most purified form of language—must be centered in a genuine gift," she argued. "The chances of getting away with
pure fakery within it are very small. One cannot fib—it shows. One cannot
manipulate—it spoils. One cannot apply decoration from the outside; or
pretend that non-feeling is feeling; or indulge in any of the lower-grade
emotions, such as self-pity" (*JAR* 68). She sought to compose the condensed lyric ("you can't be a lyric poet and love adverbs"), combining the
elements of a classical education in high school and her single year of
college with exposure to the English metaphysical poets, the French sym-
bolists, Yeats, and her catalog of Americans: "Poe (the Tales), Thoreau,
E. Dickinson and Henry James."[31] After the publication of *Body of This
Death* she immersed herself in reading Goethe, whose "intense emotion
and . . . piercing vision"[32] she believed opposed the academic formalism
that she herself repudiated. Like Goethe, she would be an "enemy of the
dry specimens of the museum."[33] With Yeats she shared a need to study the
passions, and perhaps especially compelling to her was his progression
from the naïveté and narcissism of his early romantic posture to a respon-
sive maturity. In the later Yeats she would discover a poet able "to act in the
real world and endure the results of action (responsibility the romantic hesi-
tates to assume)."[34] She valued his concision and his distrust, so similar to
her own, of "all middle grounds."[35] Although Emily Dickinson's unadul-
terated poetry would not be publicly available until 1955, Bogan closely

read and admired her poetry and acknowledged Dickinson in 1939 as one of her earliest influences.[36] After the publication of Thomas H. Johnson's edition of Dickinson's poems she became even more enthusiastic, for she discovered that the poet was "a woman of timeless genius—a visionary as well as a matchless observer of reality."[37] Both poets' omission of context, ambiguous references, and severe condensations resist our readings. And in Dickinson, Bogan saw a poet who contended with and transcribed obsessive materials.[38]

Like not only Dickinson but her contemporaries Léonie Adams and Elinor Wylie (poets with whom she was frequently compared), Bogan chose the lyric poem as her preferred medium. Her language was often simple, yet its emotional content complex. Her poems, however, are more disturbing in implication than either Wylie's or Adams's. As Babette Deutsch observed of Bogan's poems, "These poems point, more clearly than do the fastidious lyrics of Elinor Wylie or Léonie Adams, to the dark gulfs, the sheer cliffs about which the mind hovers in vain."[39] In lyric poetry Bogan would embody her conflicted relationship to her culture's mythology of romance, in which partners are not individuals with independent needs but are considered to be fused into oneness, or in which one partner is rendered subordinate to the other. The undercurrent of violence in her poems and her ironic counterpoints to the excesses of romantic love further distinguish her from many of her contemporaries. Nevertheless, Bogan shared with Wylie and Adams an unwavering fidelity to the condensed musical phrase, and she believed that the strength of the lyric as a contemporary form frequently relied on the productions of women poets. In its formal concentration, dense sound patterning, and repeated invocations and interjections, at times her poetry moved toward ritual, as Jaqueline Ridgeway has pointed out: "Form . . . is a ritualistic way of dealing with complexities that are beyond rational comprehension."[40]

Her adherence to formal poetry, stylistic compression, and a projection of female identity in the lyric place her in a lineage that includes Louise Imogen Guiney, Sara Teasdale, Lizette Woodworth Reese, and Edna St. Vincent Millay, as well as Adams and Wylie. Indeed, Bogan included all of these poets in the anthology that concluded her study *Achievement in American Poetry* and contended that the generation of women poets whose work appeared before the American public around 1918 "restored genuine and frank feeling to a literary situation which had become genteel, artificial, and dry."[41]

In her fullest discussion of form, "The Pleasures of Formal Poetry" (1953), Bogan explored two common assumptions: that traditional literary form limits expression and that form itself has been "exhausted" in modern life. Form, she contended, must be continually rejuvenated, and she cites the enlivening experiments within and outside of traditional form by Baudelaire, Rimbaud, and Mallarmé. Form, she argued, should be an area for keen experiment, opening to the refreshments of colloquial language and comic verse. She takes her major defense of formal poetry from physiology; formal poetry gives pleasure because it duplicates bodily rhythms: the heartbeat, the pulse, and the breath. In bodily rhythms poetry takes its "life," a word that reappears often in Bogan's criticism. Bogan herself approached the composition of poems in traditional form with not only a keen sense of literary history but with a preference for exact sensory reference. We might observe as well that her poetry assumes a quality of high formal tension that has led readers to refer to her poetry as if sculpture were being described. Ruth Lechlitner observed: "Her art is that of a sculptor: to fix in the 'heroic mould' the texture and motion of flesh and spirit; to capture the terrible (but corruptible) vitality and beauty of the living in deathless marble."[42] And Zabel remarked that "she *carves* the image out of the concept with scrupulous care" (emphasis mine).[43]

Bogan was to publish only three single collections; her three additional books are essentially anthologies of earlier work, supplemented by new poems. *Dark Summer*, her second book, appeared in 1929, and *The Sleeping Fury* in 1937. Subsequently, volumes of collected poems augmented by additional poems appeared. *Poems and New Poems* was published in 1941; *Collected Poems: 1923-1953* in 1954; and *The Blue Estuaries: Poems, 1923-1968* in 1968. Yet despite her relatively small oeuvre, Bogan's influence on the world of arts and letters was considerable. For thirty-eight years she served as poetry editor for the *New Yorker*. She authored a study of American literature and two other volumes of criticism and edited an anthology of children's poetry. She was also active as a translator of Goethe, Ernst Juenger, and Jules Renard. She served as Consultant in Poetry to the Library of Congress in 1945-46; received with Léonie Adams the Bollingen Prize in 1955; and was elected to the American Academy of Arts and Letters in 1969.

Although Bogan pursued the expression of private feeling, she believed that private feeling reflected cultural patterns and that contemporary poets might consolidate the modernists' gains by writing in full awareness of their historical and cultural backgrounds. In a letter of 1944 she argued, "It is time for the young writer to prove his sensitiveness by understanding what is really happening in the peculiar culture in which he finds himself. . . . [H]e can no longer spin literature out of himself, in an unrelated way."[44] She drew, however, a distinction between a poetry of politics and a poetry of culture. In her journal she asked, "What is staler than old politics? It is like walking over old furnace cinders to read what was once news of political chicanery or change" (*JAR* 97). Elsewhere, she argued that the adoption of political platforms by many writers in the 1930s was not only mistaken but indeed "more symptomatic of a spiritual *malaise* than is generally supposed."[45] In principle she rejected politics in poetry: "To sink oneself into a party is fatal, no matter how noble the tenets of that party may be. For all tenets tend to harden into dogma, and all dogma breeds hatred and bigotry, and is therefore stultifying. And the condescension of the political party toward the artist is always clear, no matter how well disguised."[46] Yet if she evaded political platforms, she did not avoid reflection upon cultural constriction. She would disapprove of the association of poets with "middle-class" values and, most especially, she would reject poetry for ideological "use." Among Victorians (and some contemporaries, she implies) "poetry was *used*: as a means of consolation, to bolster up flagging spirits, to cheer on, to cheer up; to create optimism where optimism was cheaply applied or out of place; to back up middle-class social ideals as well as certain philosophical ideals concerning human perfectibility."[47] Private feeling was not ultimately divorced, she contended, from cultural understanding. In her poems she does not present a direct portrait of her culture but projects the sensation of some of its effects, especially its effects upon women. Although her prose is grounded in historical and cultural contexts, particularly in regard to women's material and psychological conditions, in poems she portrays the experience of individual women whose desires are threatened. The threatening force that she presents is not limited to that of a romantic partner but is often figured as a peculiarly ubiquitous complex of power, suggesting both psychological and cultural impediments. It is important to note that while Bogan in her lifetime was often in rather narrow terms thought of as a love poet, her poems test romance as a conception in culture and dramatize rebellion from its limitations as a socially mandated form of negative symbiosis. In the compression and precision of her poetry she depicted the oppositions with which her culture struggled, particularly oppositions between women and men, matter and spirit, and repression and expression. Her work may claim our attention not only for its dissection of a private psychological landscape but for its power to delineate cultural assignments of meaning.

It is especially significant that Bogan would attempt to redefine a place for women poets within literary history, exploring their poetry in a way that did not create a collapse into identity with poetry written by men. Work by women of her generation, she argued, bore the separate stamp of historical circumstance and aesthetic training. As Gloria Bowles notes, Bogan was practically alone among the modern women poets "to inquire about her foremothers."[48] Bogan's 1936 essay, "Poetesses in the Parlor" offers a remarkable example of her rhetoric of difference. For in it she provides a historical overview of American women's productions as these were anthologized in the mid to the late nineteenth century, while she cumulatively suggests that the woman poet's "parlor" became a site of threat—a threat to the conventions of gender roles and gender dominance. In what she conceived to be an often lackluster field of American voices, male and female, she points out that women poets emerge in Rufus Wilmot Griswold's 1848 anthology in some variety in social class. Curiously, these poets frequently place themselves as emotional supports for their spouses, who are "frail fellows, often low in mind." Such women poets reveal their own strength in the face of their spouses' dependency. Responding to R. H. Stoddard's 1873 editing of Griswold's anthology, Bogan notes "the beginning of a critical attitude toward the married state" among new contributors.[49] She goes on to observe that the contemporary poets in Jessie F. O'Donnell's anthology of 1890, *Love Poems of Three Centuries*, effect a reversal in emotional strategies commonly associated with the sexes. "The feminine contributors positively seethe with feeling, while the passive attitude has to some extent been taken over by the males. It is the masculine voice which now assumes the tones of nostalgia and yearning, and the feminine that hymns the unfettered joys of the here-and-now."[50] She detects a "healthy assertiveness" on the women's part, for "the voices of women waiting and weeping are pretty well covered by women's voices doing nothing of the sort. And woman scorned, contrary to previous habit, now has her own remarks to make about her situation. She does not turn to flippancy and satire, like her sisters of a later date, or to faith, forgiveness, or the millrace, like betrayed members of her sex some decades earlier. She speaks out."[51] Bogan's review ends on a note that is leavened with challenge. She heralds the further development of a female poetry in America, and in quoting from a poem that expresses heated self-reflection, she observes:

> Where those sentiments had lurked hidden during the centuries since Sappho, it is difficult to say. And another frightening sound began to rise among the bamboo furniture, the Tiffany glass, from behind the framed photographs of the Coliseum and the vases of peacock feathers and pampas grass, up from beneath carved table and chair legs: the voice of the possessive woman, loud enough to penetrate beyond the grave.

From women's enclosed space, the traditional middle-class home with its predictable interior decoration, "something remarkable," a "final and alarming result," arises, which would seem all to the good in the context of Bogan's argument.[52] Rather than dismissing the mass of nineteenth-century women's poetry in America—most of it, if not reviled, roundly forgotten by this time—Bogan ascribes to some of the poetry an uncanny power in which women assume the emotional provinces and rhetorical strategies previously assigned to men. For our discussion, it may be especially noteworthy that although she places women within a domestic site, the parlor, from their familiar material conditions she allows nineteenth-century women's poetry to threaten conventions of representation.

In her critical study *Achievement in American Poetry* Bogan argues that women changed the tone of American poetry at the turn of the century through the "task" of "revivifying warmth of feeling." As she observed, "This task, it is now evident, was accomplished almost entirely by women poets through methods which proved to be as strong as they seemed to be delicate."[53] In a climate of derision and in a context in which women were perceived as a flawed deviation from a masculine norm, she praised her female predecessors' strengths and applauded their very "break" with convention. "If they begin their break with some of the naive gestures of the amateur, they were to conclude it with the full invigorating knowledge of the ways and means of the artist."[54] At the same time, she was not comfortable with efforts to divide the sexes within anthologies, although her own critical writing examined women and men for the separate conditions from which their poetry arose. With a flippancy that repulsed some of her critics, she declined in a 1935 letter to edit an anthology of women poets: "The thought of corresponding with a lot of female songbirds made me acutely ill. It is hard enough to bear with my own lyric side." At the same time, she submitted a poem to the women's anthology in the *New Republic*. If she would not edit the anthology, she nevertheless insisted upon joining the ranks of the other women in the anthology. And she went to considerable trouble to do so, writing a lengthily apologetic letter to John Hall Wheelock in an attempt to withdraw "Italian Morning" from publication in order to submit it to the *New Republic*. "I would like to see it in the N.R., as a kind of proud gesture against the Malcolm Cowleys, the Kenneth Burkes and the Bruce Blivens of this world."[55] Her own anthology of American verse, published as an appendix in *Achievement in American Poetry*, remains unusual to this day for its relatively broad inclusion of women poets: eleven women against a total of nineteen men.

In a sympathetic review of *A Room of One's Own*, Bogan not only echoes Virginia Woolf but urges her contemporaries to avoid internalizing "ponderous masculine judgment" and to resist "tiresome gestures of romantic escape":

They should look upon reality with that fixity, that wit, that honorable just-
ness of proportion, which can be so characteristically female, not hesitating
to state what, as women, they feel on any subject, and passing over as not to
the point any ponderous masculine judgment passed upon them. For if
women's work in fiction, and in literature in general, has, up to the present,
been marred by touches of hysteria and sentimentality, it must be remembered that, as opposed to men's work in literature, as in any other field, there
are fewer examples of it. Women, one might add, urged, as Mrs. Woolf urges
them, to solid work in literature, philosophy, history and the sciences, need
not worry about hysterical lapses in the presentation of their findings, if they
look critically at the hysteria implicit in Rousseau's passion for social re-
form, Shelley's poetry, Novalis' mysticism, Schopenhauer's philosophy and
the terrific compensatory historical bias of Carlyle. They may trust that their
work will in time and through travail become increasingly perfect and whole,
and enter into a full period of production, free at once of their former bitterness in subjection, and of their present rather tiresome gestures of romantic
escape.[56]

When writing of women poets, Bogan was keenly aware that she confronted a critical situation that at times was openly hostile. She herself was
a rigorous critic of women's productions rather than simply an affirmative
presence. Indeed, she rhetorically allotted a constraining place to both sexes.
Yet in assigning weaknesses to women writers, she denies them fluency
with those qualities that she does not highly prize in the lyric: a command
of abstraction and a mastery of certain traditional structures, notably the
five-act play, a form that she finds, at any rate, obsolete. In "The Heart and
the Lyre" (1947) she asks, "Why should women, past, present, or future,
remain fixed in the determination to out-Shakespeare Shakespeare? Can it
be that there is no basic reason for women to excel in the art of poetry by
producing the same sort of structure as men? Men, as a matter of fact,
stayed with the five-act poetic tragedy far too long. Perhaps women have
more sense than to linger over an obsessing form of this kind."[57] She praises
what she herself struggled to develop and most valued in women's poetry:
lyric intensity and the pursuit of a language for feeling. Elsewhere she
argued, "All art, in spite of the struggles of some critics to prove otherwise,
is based on emotion and projects emotion" (*JAR* 120). Portions of her essays often have been used as evidence of Bogan's presumed suspicion of
women's capacity as writers, and yet her essays in their entirety reflect her
hopes of persuading a resistant audience of the value of much of women's
writing. In context, her ascriptions of women's failures are often rhetorical
inoculations amid her celebration of women's capacity. Women were not
"required" by their culture to master abstraction, yet while she finds women

less likely than men to pursue and command abstractions, she goes on to point out that women "often experiment boldly with form and language"[58] and that they "are capable of perfect and poignant song."[59] She urges women to avoid internalizing negative judgments of their gender, declaring that women must resist "an imitation of certain masculine 'trends' in contemporary poetry" and advising them to avoid overestimating "the work of male verbalizers and poetic logicians."[60] She suggests that women withstand "contemporary pressures or mistaken self consciousness."[61] It was in emotion, and most especially in the lyric, that she believed the women poets of her generation discovered their power. The lyric poem, the poem that earned her greatest admiration, must be profoundly based in emotion. "In women," she argued, "more than in men, the intensity of their emotions is the key to the treasures of their spirit."[62] Her sympathy and her loyalty remained with outsiders, women among them, who defeated convention through indirection and subversion, as she argued in *Achievement in American Poetry*: "The history of the American arts from 1900 on is often a record of successful flank attacks made by 'outsiders' upon an entrenchment of taste and techniques against which straight-forward frontal attacks would have failed."[63]

In this study I shall be paying special attention to the themes of obsession and release, among the primary psychic activities that Bogan's work charts. Obsession is portrayed as excessive preoccupation with betrayal in love and with psychological engulfment. She was in turn interested in exploring preoccupying memories and intuitions of early childhood incidents that appeared to her to have been partly effaced from her own consciousness. She investigates the "contours" of obsessive fears and desires, particularly as her speakers are threatened by unnamed forces, culturally and psychologically positioned to deny the speakers' "breath," and thus their art. Increasingly beset by her own imaginative silences after 1937, Bogan sought to dramatize the process of gradual release from obsessive fears of betrayal and entrapment. In the late poems her haunted psyches are supplanted by those released from threats of domination as she reimagines a sense of being, shifting outward to consider receptivity toward natural processes. She imagines release from all physical constraints, an iridescence of being and a widening of horizons beyond the narcissistic concerns of the ego. Her speakers reexamine their pasts and newly name and possess aspects of female selfhood.

In my own rereading of Bogan's poetry, particularly in focusing on those poems that investigate and embody repression, I necessarily refer at different points to the writings of Sigmund Freud, for Bogan was at least

an informal student of psychoanalytic literature and had undergone psychoanalysis for many years, apparently as early as 1922.[64] Bogan's desire to
understand the unconscious appears to have been strong even in later life.
One of her later projects, for instance, involved an attempt to conceptual-
ize the id. Yet her most sustained focus on the unconscious appears most
satisfactorily derived from the very process of writing. She found Freudian
theory to be suggestive rather than confining, a matter for brief forays rather
than extended or slavish adherence, and I have attempted to make note of
her references to Freudianism in a similar spirit. In pursuing close readings
of her poetry I have found particularly illuminating the theories of Julia
Kristeva and, in somewhat briefer form, those of Margaret Homans, the
latter drawing upon Jacques Lacan and Nancy Chodorow.

Writing to her publisher in 1936, Bogan offered suggestions for cover
copy on her third book, pointing out that not only did she care about "effects of tension, sonority, etc. that *language* can produce" but that any
"blurb" should emphasize, "that our unconscious (Uncs., in Freud's charm-
ing phraseology) knows more about us than we know about it."[65] For Bogan
the unconscious is most often figured spatially, following in large measure
Freud's early topographical model. In her poems it may be figured as a
region, a house, or a room. For Bogan the unconscious is an uncannily
reflective sphere, replicating its own errors, as from the subject's childhood it develops structures:

> To trace the dream-landscape that has grown inside me every night, all
> my life, along with daylight reality, and which has mountains, ruins, islands,
> shores, cities, and even *suburbs* and summer "resorts" *of its own*, related to
> one another and, many times, recurrent (almost in the sense of revisited).
>   It has its gardens, its hills, and its sea. Other than ours. A reflection; a
> distortion. . . . And it repeats its mistakes, as though it had learned them by
> rote. . . . (*JAR* 173)

Bogan not only draws upon intuitions about the existence of the unconscious but molds some of her poems in the image of the unconscious as she
understood it—as peculiarly resistant to conventional meaning and cease-
lessly duplicating "accidents" of memory. She was, as I shall argue, especially interested in exploring repression. "The repressed becomes the poem"
(*JAR* 72) Bogan wrote, and in this context I am using the term *repression* to
refer to material normally inaccessible to consciousness that may nevertheless be insinuated through the complex workings of a poem. The unconscious by definition cannot be mastered, but for Bogan the achieved poem
may elicit intimations of unconscious processes. In the images and dramas

of her poems Bogan at times duplicates two of the "characteristics" that Freud ascribed to the processes of the unconscious: *"timelessness,* and *replacement of external by psychical reality."*[66] Moments are seen (in Theodore Roethke's words about Bogan's poem "Medusa") "under the sheer sky of eternity"[67]—in a timeless sphere—and images of nature are rendered symbolic of psychic reality.

In particular her poems are marked by her fidelity to the promptings of the unconscious as it may be affected by a certain order of feminine experience in North American culture. Bogan asserted that the dynamics of women's psyches were ignored, and a model based on exclusively masculine psychology dominated critical discussion. She charged that women's "psychic processes operate according to rules which have never been fully discovered or explored."[68] Her complex position in regard to gender led Kenneth Rexroth to refer to Bogan as a "militant feminist and 'free woman.'" Insightfully, he observed that much of her work proves "either a celebration of her womanhood or intensely, but cryptically erotic."[69]

The power to write well, rather than facilely, Bogan asserted, depended upon factors beyond conscious control. "It [inspiration] comes and goes; it cannot be forced and it can very rarely be summoned up by the conscious will" (*JAR* 119). And yet the poem, originating from the unconscious, that distorted and distorting "country," must submit to the tension of the poet's craft. The route to the poem begins in unconscious processes, she believed, but it is only completed when counterpoised by a highly evolved sense of form.

My first chapter discusses the ways in which Bogan inaugurates her career by making explicit the "productive violence" that Julia Kristeva attributes to literary texts. Through her emphasis on violent separation Bogan focuses on alienation between the sexes. She appropriates the myth of Daphne to dramatize a central crisis: the female assaulted by ubiquitous cultural force serves as a figure for the poet.

My second chapter explores repression and secrecy in *Dark Summer*. Rupturing events, discussed in the first chapter, are followed by Bogan's focus on the experience of psychological containment. She examines the state of repression itself, a state that—as Hélène Cixous provocatively asserts—produces a "place" for women. Bogan investigates withheld grief as she figures the effects of repression. Yet even as the poems delineate the territory of repression and "span the limit" of its origin, they testify to the difficulty of progressing beyond confined energies.

The third chapter examines Bogan's subsequent recovery of the maternal in *The Sleeping Fury*. The poems of her third book cast the mother as a source of creativity and enact a recognition of maternal power. The poems' personae duplicate maternal experience and examine scenes of order and disorder in ways that allude to the mother.

The poems appearing after Bogan's publication of her three individual collections present peculiar challenges to her readers, for Bogan casts new images of luminosity and psychic release during decades in which she endured sustained imaginative silences. In the fourth chapter my analysis of the poems draws attention to the luminous diffusion of poems and personae. In her late career she produced poetry of compelling distinction that affronted her own severe self-censor and contributed to her position as an extraordinary lyric poet and a major modernist.

As Louise Bogan's poetry continues to be read, we may more fully observe the ways in which it assumes provocative status. In what had once seemed a cool and rigidly ordered art, presenting a closed face and a brittle completion, we may detect not only a poetry profoundly shaped by female experiences in Western culture but a poetry profoundly questioning orders of female experience. It is a poetry that both explores the shape of one female unconscious and points to a culture's most deeply rooted obsessions.

1

Violence and Difference:
Body of This Death

Body of This Death (1923) is Louise Bogan's most violent book of poetry. It is violent in its opposition to physical, emotional, and spiritual constraint; violent in its investigations of conceptual dualities; and violent in its images of breakage. Her personae declare their desires to withstand coercion of any sort, and they reject, at the same time, harmonious affinities. An impulse toward sexual and emotional chastity as a feminine ideal is ironically defeated ("Ad Castitatem"); romantic transport is reduced ("Betrothed"); and the mastery of feminine energy appears illusory ("The Frightened Man," "The Romantic"). In Bogan's first book verbal models of rupture oppose the ubiquitous threat of violation that would suppress her speaker's very breath and, inevitably, her art. Her opponents would seem, purposefully, to be rendered amorphous as complexes of cultural force.

The book is balanced between two modes: the testing of desires in "A Tale," "The Alchemist," and "Ad Castitatem"; and the rejection of an obscured but palpable source of persecution, as in "Statue and Birds" and "Fifteenth Farewell." The reenvisioned desire and the repulsed violation characterize Bogan's first collection.

Body of This Death begins with an account of innocence transformed by dreadful experience. In portraying a determined search for changelessness, Bogan writes a morality tale, since such a quest must inevitably fail. First published in the *New Republic* in October 1921, "A Tale" dramatizes a youth's wish to break from his native environment. His actions, emphasizing rupture ("He cuts what holds his days together"), are those that Bogan will investigate for both genders. But in rendering her quest figure as masculine, although she most often would go on to write self-consciously of women, she both inaugurates her career with a failed masculine search and announces her authority to formulate aesthetic quests that transcend gender:

31

This youth too long has heard the break
Of waters in a land of change.
He goes to see what suns can make
From soil more indurate and strange.

He cuts what holds his days together
And shuts him in, as lock on lock:
The arrowed vane announcing weather,
The tripping racket of a clock;

Seeking, I think, a light that waits
Still as a lamp upon a shelf,—
A land with hills like rocky gates
Where no sea leaps upon itself.

But he will find that nothing dares
To be enduring, save where, south
Of hidden deserts, torn fire glares
On beauty with a rusted mouth,—

Where something dreadful and another
Look quietly upon each other.

                                                (*BE* 3)

The youth, we learn immediately, desires a permanent form of order. Nevertheless, to evade "the break / Of waters in a land of change" he must engage in yet more ruptures, shattering his connection to one climate and the flow of time. The natural landscape the youth seeks is reduced metaphorically to that of human-made structures, to a room with its lamp and to a gated space. The sea that "leaps" upon itself is further enclosed, mirroring bodily imagery, the flow of blood and the self-defeating activity of obsessive sexual passions.

Finally, the youth's projected utopia harbors monsters, for "torn fire glares / On beauty with a rusted mouth." Imagistically these lines are remarkably complex. Is desire itself a "torn fire" with "a rusted mouth"? Or is beauty, in the syntactic ambiguity of these lines, the possessor of "a rusted mouth"? In the density of her images, Bogan creates a treacherous equation: all that "dares / To be enduring" is nevertheless stalled by obsessive desire. What lasts—if lasting order could be possible and apprehensible—would be a realm of ravaging fire. If the torn fire is itself a rusted mouth, such a mouth must be unable to speak, and passion, in being torn, has succumbed to some form of violence. Here passion and beauty both are mute as the poem ends with a drama of sight that freezes, however quietly, its monstrous sphinxlike pairing.

The poem's concluding couplet does not suggest recognition so much as merging; the poem's monstrous selves are undifferentiated. "Something dreadful and another" are locked in permanent and fruitless contest. The very amorphous qualities of these forms and their near-linguistic identity reinforce our sense of their inseparability. The concluding lines initiate the pose that Bogan will assume. She too will be dreadful—in dread of her own coercion by the psyche's phantoms and, as we shall see, her culture's coercions. In turn, she will come to incite a form of dread in some of her readers as a poet in command of austere compression, for the poem would seem watertight in its masterful quatrains, alternating rhymes, insistent stresses—and resistance to simple explication. Yet Bogan's considerable formal talents in this tetrameter lyric should not obscure the implicit violence of her poetics, a poetics marked by the will to investigate and disrupt stasis of the sort that "A Tale" projects. The poem surely not only absorbs the images of Bogan's youth (the rush of waters in mill towns of her childhood and the "soil more indurate and strange" of the Panama Canal Zone where her early marriage failed) but, more important, it points toward discovery through failure. Her young people are often experimentalists whose lessons are deeply ambiguous, for if we ask the poem's major question— "What dares to be enduring?"—at least two answers arise. If the static forms at the close of the poem are monstrous representations of the psyche's paralysis, we enter into a realm that we might associate with the mythic or, given the poem's sinister shadings, the gothic. But we might also answer the question of "what dares to be enduring" by replying that the poem itself dares. The final vision that the poem projects, then, would be of poetry itself, the sort that Bogan at this time puts before us: a poetry that seeks to endure through dislocations and ruptures, and by displaying seemingly irreconcilable figures.

Apparently the poem's complexities continued to appear meaningful to Bogan, a notoriously stern critic of her own work, throughout her career. She chose to reprint "A Tale" as the introductory poem in her final three collections. She chose, then, to make it her recurrent beginning as a signature piece indicating her willingness to examine obsessive desire.

Body of This Death is framed by the quest motif of "A Tale" and, at its conclusion, by the triumphantly resistant "Sonnet." Considering the poems together is a useful exercise, for, by establishing the limits of the book as such, Bogan points to glaring paralysis and abrupt divisions as her speakers attempt to remove themselves from a field of force that threatens them.

The poems allude to violence contained within both order and disorder: the seemingly stalled order of psychic paralysis and the sudden disruptions of experience. In turn, she presents symbolic counterviolence, a willed effort to defeat personal and cultural inhibitions by turning violence back upon its source. "Sonnet" addresses not only its eponymous traditional form but an unidentified power that threatens to possess the speaker:

> Since you would claim the sources of my thought
> Recall the meshes whence it sprang unlimed,
> The reedy traps which other hands have timed
> To close upon it . . .
> .   .   .   .
>
> My mouth, perhaps, may learn one thing too well,
> My body hear no echo save its own,
> Yet will the desperate mind, maddened and proud,
> Seek out the storm, escape the bitter spell
> That we obey, strain to the wind, be thrown
> Straight to its freedom in the thunderous cloud.

(*BE* 26)

As in a poem that we will discuss shortly, "Statue and Birds," the features of the speaker's opponent are not described. Nevertheless, this violating other appears as a restrictive agent of convention who would deny the speaker's value and "claim" the origins of her conceptions. The one addressed, however, becomes only a witness to the speaker's freedom rather than a final impediment. "Whatever nets draw in to prison me / At length your eyes must turn to watch it go." As Sara Via Pais has noted, impediments may actually energize this headstrong persona: "The conflict is clear; but so is the sense that the will and energy of the self are released by brushes with entrapment, and that a necessary tension exists between the 'desperate mind, maddened and proud,' and the things that menace it. For they do not only threaten, they also galvanize. In reaction to them the self is flung into freedom."[1] In part, Bogan defines her authority through opposition, challenging her own talents by adopting the demanding requirements of the Italian sonnet and declaring her intent to master formal constraints. She avoids a simplistic romantic figuration of a Greenwich Village stripe, perhaps the expected antagonist for a young woman poet in the 1920s, but more broadly intimates a complex of force that would be drawn from her cultural milieu or from poetic tradition. Purposefully, it seems, she renders her opponent as diffuse, as if the obstacles to her speaker's fulfillment inevitably could not be localized in one place.

"Statue and Birds" (*BE* 14), first published in the *New Republic* in April 1922, serves as a further introduction to a recurrent theme of obscure menace in this poetry. At the poem's center, in a "withered arbor," a statue "stands . . . with hands flung out in alarm / Or remonstrances." The poem is reminiscent of the Daphne-Apollo myth, for in attempting to escape Apollo as cultural authority and male law, Daphne (like the statue in Bogan's poem) is rendered mute and immobile. Although the statue might represent a host of mythological figures of powerless women, Bogan's metaphors centering on trees and woods allude to Daphne at the moment of her transformation into the laurel: "woods rake on the sky," and "the inquietudes of the sap . . . are spent." While the cause of the girl's paralysis is not visible, tellingly the statue is enclosed in phallic representations: "the woven bracts of the vine" move "in a pattern of angles"; "the quill of the fountain falters"; pheasants reveal "arrowy wings" and "sharp tails." In such a bristling and angular environment, the quail and pheasants that "walk by slowly, circling the girl" may likewise become a hunter's victims.

The cause of the girl's distress is not named or in any way rendered explicit. Yet as the girl's posture of frozen flight suggests, the absence of any representation of her opponent does not defeat Apollo's actual influence. This implacable and pervasive other need not be visible to be experienced. His paralyzing effect is felt throughout the girl's world. The poem's insistent pauses, marked by six commas in the first quatrain alone, reinforce our sense of arrested motion. The use of modifying elements, more pronounced than usual in this period of Bogan's career, further slows the poem. The fountain itself is metaphorically allied to the pen, for it is a *quill* that *falters*, signifying that the anxiety at the center of this arbor reflects that of the poet herself, frozen into immobility.

Taken together, the marble statue of the girl, the "golden quails," and the ritualistic patterning convey the stillness of a frieze. The girl, carved in marble, most clearly serves as a warning sign of disaster through her physical and psychological paralysis. Her pose of anxiety is, after all, perpetual. Both Elizabeth Frank and Deborah Pope view the poem as Bogan's objection to artifice. As Frank argues, "Art must be freed from its prison of form to leave 'the withered arbor' of artifice."[2] Pope sees the statue as "representative of women fixed by art as well as by artificiality, unable by 'definition'— that is, statue, myth, pedestal, art—to express themselves."[3] Nevertheless, I would argue, a distinction should be made, for the poem does not oppose artifice itself so much as protest the lack of competing artificialities. The girl's tragedy is not simply that she has been "fixed by art" and artifice; Bogan, after all, was unwavering in her admiration of formal properties in poems. Rather, the marble girl's tragedy is that she has not freely impelled her own transformation but has been metamorphosed as a response to acute danger. Here the too-powerful artifice of Apollo as not only god of law but god of poetry must be controverted by another powerful artifice that is outwardly directed, an artifice that Bogan will laboriously attempt to construct throughout much of her career.

In this context, Daphne's myth serves most fully as a means of dramatizing a central crisis: the female assaulted by a seemingly superior force proves a figure for the poet who may be threatened by the strictures of an alien art—the art of Apollo as god of poetry in a tradition principally defined and judged by men. In the marble girl Bogan delineates at least a partial response. The girl must assume a position of protest and opposition, a characteristic gesture within Bogan's early poetry. Repeatedly, Bogan presents speakers who reveal through their physical postures their resistance to an authority that would deny them even so much as living bodily presence.

For Bogan, the issue of transformation as escape from coercion is itself, however, suspect. After all, Daphne, her principal figure of transformation, metamorphoses into an inferior state. If Daphne is transformed into the laurel, a sign of achievement for others, Daphne is herself defeated. She becomes the symbolic reward rather than the one rewarded; her transformation renders her into ornament and sign, object rather than subject. As Bogan wrote suggestively in a 1939 review of the mythological figure characterized by transformation, "there are better gods than Proteus."[4]

"Stanza" (*BE* 21), first printed in *Measure* in November 1922, sheds further light on Bogan's allusion to ubiquitous restraint that permeates an environment. Once again, Bogan casts doubt upon the authority of transformation as it is practiced by or against the disempowered. In a certain sense the poem is a lament for poetic decline, recording a young poet's fears of an ebb in power. Elizabeth Frank argues, "Bogan makes it clear that even her first exhilarating encounters with inspiration have resolved themselves into the disaffection of experience."[5] Yet perhaps the poem's most disturbing implications center on repudiating myths of violent transformations as these are visited upon women. In "Stanza" mortal women annul godhead. Indeed, the poem's final image renders godly transformation into nullity or waste:

> The eyes that opened to white day
> Watch cloud that men may look upon:
> Leda forgets the wings of the swan;
> Danaë has swept the gold away.

> (*BE* 21)

Another poetic, one of divine metamorphoses and of men's power over women, is dismissed as Bogan overturns a mythology of patriarchal inspiration. Women coerced by godhead, like the girl of "Statue and Birds," are now disenthralled from structures of authority. The final domestic image in which we see Danaë wield her broom supplants the image of the alien impregnating moment. In Bogan's work, as we shall see in the next chapter, Leda's forgetfulness and Danaë's sweeping imply a desire for destruction of negative psychical material. Here the women's actions suggest another strategy in the aftermath of their possession: a positive self-cleansing rather than transformation. The poem's title, "Stanza," suggests a room in its etymology; poetic space becomes women's space. While the image of "the hands that seized / Small wreaths from branches scarcely green" recalls Apollonian hands, such godly hands here have been thrust aside.

While Bogan writes of women paralyzed by encounters with powerful others, her opponent—if female—is often confronted and recognized. Essential differences exist, for instance, between "Statue and Birds" and one of her best-known poems, "Medusa" (to be discussed at length in chapter 3), in which female power is fully viewed. Unlike the girl of "Statue and Birds," the speaker of "Medusa" observes her antagonist, tells her own story, and assumes the primary bearing and behavior of the overwhelming other in a moment of identification. Contrastingly, "Statue and Birds" creates an impression of immobility alone, unmodified by recognition or an assumption of identity with an antagonist. As law and patriarchal tradition, Apollo remains expressly other and antagonistic.

A depiction of resistance to alien presences is one of the most common elements of Bogan's early work. In fact, Theodore Roethke, who had known Bogan for a short time as a lover and later as his mentor and friend, described her as "a contender, an opponent, an adversary."[6] Such contention, whether its suggested embodiment is female or male, assumes the status of a working practice, as in "Fifteenth Farewell," in which her speaker addresses constraining force: "You may have all things from me, save my breath, / The slight life in my throat will not give pause / For your love, nor your loss, nor any cause" (*BE* 24). Ultimately, Bogan's speaker voices her refusal to succumb to any limitations upon her powers.

Given Bogan's fierce independence, it is important to note that metaphors of violent activity—as a means of securing and displaying independence—run throughout much of her poetry, most emphatically in *Body of This Death*. Certainly Bogan employs the word "beat" as a musical and rhythmical notation; she went so far as to complain in her correspondence of her reliance on the word. Yet we should note that she repeats the word in contexts that suggest a counterviolence that may fracture the immobilized double and separate the self from coercive others or complexes of force. In *Body of This Death*, things, and passions, are bent, cracked, torn, broken, or shattered. To assume forceful feeling through forceful measures, she focuses on "beating" repeatedly. To free the image from deadening context, she would "beat out the image whole." In "Sub Contra," for instance, the beat opposes the "whimper":

> Let there sound from music's root
> One note rage can understand,
> A fine noise of riven things.
> Build there some thick chord of wonder;
> Then, for every passion's sake,
> Beat upon it till it break.

> (*BE* 5)

She asks for "A fine noise of riven things," the poem as continual and audible rupture. Ultimately, "Sub Contra" addresses the fear that inspiration eventually might be muted, yet the solution it presents is rage. Passion, specifically "every passion," requires a new shattering of meaning. The resulting tone is one of rousing ambition, the final rhyming lines, a couplet in a poem otherwise without near end rhymes, forms a seal, a correspondence through which the final word *break* accumulates force. As if to duplicate the conceptual weight of rupture even down to the seemingly lower-order matters of punctuation, seventeen of the book's twenty-seven poems include at least one dash, seldom to mimic effects of hesitation, but more often serving through the effect of interruption to heighten the material following the dash and to create an impression of renewed intensity.

In departing from images of the cruelly petrified woman, Bogan urges that resistance to oppressive force, whatever its source or form, be newly imagined. As Carol Moldaw observes, "'Sub Contra' expresses the desire for an aesthetic form which will exemplify, or even create a heightened state of emotion."[7] The "heightened state of emotion" toward which the poem aspires is marked by repeated fractures. In a manner that may illuminate Bogan's explorations, Julia Kristeva has ascribed to literary texts a quality of "productive violence":

If there exists a "discourse" which is not a mere depository of thin linguistic layers, an archive of structures, or the testimony of a withdrawn body, and is, instead, the essential element of a practice involving the sum of unconscious, subjective, and social relations in gestures of confrontation and appropriation, destruction and construction—productive violence, in short—it is "literature," or, more specifically the *text*.[8]

By putting forward Kristeva's description of the literary text's "productive violence," I wish to emphasize that Bogan overtly creates oppositions without resolutions. Most often she is less interested in transforming images or rendering them fluid in relationship to one another than in posing extreme juxtapositions between images and actions and in insinuating collisions within the psyche. Her work is a "practice" of sorts, defined in part by the elements that Kristeva ascribes to the literary text: "gestures of confrontation, and appropriation, destruction and construction." While all of these elements are evident in Bogan's work, among its distinguishing features is the very prevalence of explicit acts of confrontation and destruction or, more specifically in the latter instance, of "appropriated destruction." That is, the underbeat that we detect in her poetry is itself a manipulation of the gestures of cultural law. The power of the Apollonian authority who may immobilize the poet is countered by a repeated command: "Break."

In a somewhat later poem, "Cassandra" (*BE* 33), first published in the *Nation* in December 1924, Bogan explicitly writes of the lyric cry as violent. In an eight-line stanza of alternate rhymes she makes Cassandra, like the "fury" of her third book, an inciting presence whose madness is a kind of knowledge inseparable from her isolation. Like Daphne, Cassandra is also Apollo's victim, her prophecies cursed by Apollo to be disbelieved. Yet it is not the disaster she foretells so much as the very act of speech that preoccupies this speaker, not the content of her speech so much as recognition of the disruptive power projected by her own voice as a dismissed prophet, a position of particular significance for the woman poet. Adopting an opposite position to Daphne, Cassandra is "shrieking" rather than dumb. In this mythological figure Bogan makes manifest the essential violence of her poetic. Language performs oppositionally; it is itself a violence (a "wing" that "tears"). Indeed, the "wing" that "tears" will be echoed decades later in Bogan's late poem "The Daemon," in which a woman is compelled to speak of the origin of her inspiration: "The bruise in the side." In "Cassandra" the poet must herself, at the moment that she perceives violence, recognize a culture's "tricks of lust and pride."

> Song, like a wing, tears through my breast, my side,
> And madness chooses out my voice again,
> Again. I am the chosen no hand saves:

> The shrieking heaven lifted over men,
> Not the dumb earth, wherein they set their graves.

> (*BE* 33)

Cassandra denigrates a hierarchy of traditional authority and, like Leda and Danaë, disrupts allegiance to a male divine. Through Cassandra, Bogan projects a furious alter ego who reverses the traditional dyad uniting women and earth, men and sky, and creates her own apotheosis as "the shrieking heaven." Cassandra purveys the voice of urgent life rather than an earth of "dumb" graves. Her role is to create the poem as prophecy: "I am the chosen no hand saves."

Bogan meets cultural violence, whether such violence denigrates its Cassandras or paralyzes its female poets, with violence of feeling and an enactment of revolt. In discussing "Cassandra," Elizabeth Frank notes that "from its hidden source poetry creates speech which is profoundly *other* and *opposed* to the received notions of men."[9] If the myth of Daphne and Apollo serves as Bogan's voicing of crisis in the face of power, the power of patriarchal presence embodied in Apollo as law, Bogan further dramatizes the inadequacy of capitulation to cultural consensus in "Cassandra." Her reputation as a poet of austerity and reserve may obscure the innate turbulence of her vision. Yet in the oppositional sphere of her poetry, she chooses a role similar to Cassandra's, for whom "song, like a wing, tears"; through the intensity of her language Bogan would assume an aesthetics of violence and difference.

A somewhat later and initially rather puzzling poem may prove illuminating in this context. In "I Saw Eternity," first published in 1929 in *Dark Summer*, Bogan records her impatience with even so much as the romantic poet's traditional desire for immortality. Although Cheryl Walker, for one, finds the poem to be extreme in its implications ("madness may be seen lurking at the edges of a poem about overly acute sensitivities"),[10] the poem is more clearly, as Bogan herself posited, cathartic.[11] The poem alludes to Henry Vaughan's "The World" ("I saw Eternity the other night / Like a great *Ring* of pure and endless light"), but Bogan subverts her seventeenth-century source's Christian piety. In the poem she challenges her own desires for immortality, not only in terms of her early exposure to the dogma of the Catholic Church, but perhaps more fully in light of the romantic pursuit of immortality through the writing of literature. The conception of the poet's immortality, she suggests, must submit to creative destruction:

> O beautiful Forever!
> O grandiose Everlasting!

Now, now, now,
I break you into pieces,
I feed you to the ground.

O brilliant, O languishing
Cycle of weeping light!
The mice and birds will eat you,
And you will spoil their stomachs
As you have spoiled my mind.

Here, mice, rats,
Porcupines and toads,
Moles, shrews, squirrels,
Weasels, turtles, lizards,—
Here's bright Everlasting!
Here's a crumb of Forever!
Here's a crumb of Forever!

(*BE* 50)

In this poem, the abstract timelessness that threatened to ruin the youth of "A Tale" is dismantled in favor of flux. With its strong parallels and ironically inflated adjectives and capitalizations, the poem rejects an order of ambition that Bogan found stultifying. The "grandiose," the target of Cassandra's astringent prophesies, is savaged and returned to living actuality.

As we have seen, separation rather than unity defines this poetics. To disengage from oppressive elements within and outside the self, Bogan creates images and acts of division and rupture that might in some ways account for critical unease toward her work. Her poetry is itself a form of criticism in its avidness for distinctions. Unless we invert our usual categories of response, her poems will repel our readings. Separation, rather than unity, is a perceived necessity, a necessity that has consequences for the ways in which we may read and respond to this poetry. Her emphasis on willed breakage of all sorts amounts to a determined effort to unsettle conventional patterns of representation.

In the early poem, "The Alchemist," for instance, elements of separation and disaffiliation are dramatized. In the poem, an alchemist-poet experiments through a willed separation between body and mind in an effort to convert the gross substances of her experience into gold. When the alchemist's experiment fails to meet her expectations, she newly discovers "unmysterious flesh":

I burned my life, that I might find
A passion wholly of the mind,

> Thought divorced from eye and bone,
> Ecstasy come to breath alone.
> I broke my life, to seek relief
> From the flawed light of love and grief.
>
> With mounting beat the utter fire
> Charred existence and desire.
> It died low, ceased its sudden thresh.
> I had found unmysterious flesh—
> Not the mind's avid substance—still
> Passionate beyond the will.

(*BE* 15)

Curiously, the alchemist's rediscovery of her flesh proves her reward; by attempting to sever mind from body she is once again returned to the base and province of her desires. The poem's two six-line stanzas emphasize the inevitability of her "failure" through the regularity of the tetrameter couplets. The first-person pronoun is insistently placed at the openings of three lines as if to emphasize the poem's status as an exercise in identity testing. Most important, through the poem Bogan opposes the cultural repudiation of the body and, as a consequence, the cultural rejection of women's bodily selves as desiring subjects. If in dyadic thinking the flesh is allied with the feminine, the very insolubility of the flesh in "The Alchemist" suggests, at last, a victory for the feminine itself. The final reassertion of the body in this and other poems frequently amounts to a triumph for not only physical desire but for the feminine as it has been culturally aligned with the body. In other poems that ironically invite chastity and at least superficially dispel eroticism ("Ad Castitatem," "My Voice Not Being Proud"), Bogan characterizes the flesh as a female realm that resists coercive transformation. As an alchemy of sorts, her depiction of extremes is carried out experimentally. The acts of extraction and externalization serve as aesthetic strategies that apply pressure to conventional dichotomies. At moments, Bogan's poems flare into near-transcendent passages; yet, finally, they return to celebrate the enabling formal constraints that the body may provide.

As I observed in the introduction, Bogan's confidence in traditional form (if not in traditional cultural consensus) rested largely on her belief that it duplicates the body's rhythms. She insisted on a formal poetry that has a physiological basis, linked to the body's rhythm and pulse.[12] The vocabulary of images in her poetry is based in some measure on the body. Each image, whether of hand, eye, mouth, heart, or tongue, is embedded into the poem as if to make emphatic the materiality of the body. Her affirmation of the body assumes renewed meaning if we consider her first book's title and epigraph, taken from Paul's Epistle to the Romans: "Who shall deliver me from the body of this death?" Deborah Pope finds the epigraph to be a "touching and relatively unguarded cry against necessity and her youthful determination to avoid life's traps."[13] Jaqueline Ridgeway and Elizabeth Frank connect the epigraph not only to Romans but to *The Symbolist Movement in Literature,* in which Arthur Symons refers to Baudelaire's rebellion against "the mere literature of words." The title line, Ridgeway observes, suggests "the weight of words on the artist's aspiration to expression as well as Paul's weight of sin on the soul's aspiration to goodness."[14] Most often Bogan sought to explore passions in her poetry without being naïvely exploited by the cultural mandates of romantic love, and in turn she represents death as itself a body, "the body of this death." Her cry for deliverance from the body of death suggests, once again, a separation, and certainly in this context it is important to note that the book's title intimates violence. The body of construction and destruction is insinuated. The book of poems itself becomes the body: the substance of testimony that recounts and alternately enacts petrifaction and severance.

The aesthetic and conceptual technique of separation, especially as it affects the gendered body, is particularly evident in Bogan's most controversial poem. If a body of work could be said to contain a culprit, "Women" is Bogan's most perversely seductive culprit. Readings of the poem have contributed to a calcified presentation of Bogan's poetics as inimical to women. In a number of ways, the poem refuses a stable position, accounting for a plethora of contradictory readings. The poem has been seen as a burlesque of gender, a broadside of self-hatred, a celebration of difference, a critique of culture, a disguised rebuttal to men, and a savage criticism of women. No doubt the poem retains its power because it holds such possibilities in tension, refracting its conceptual hues broadly for each reader. Unfortunately, the poem is seldom acknowledged as a conceptual victory, even though it proves a remarkably accomplished appropriation of a censorious cultural voice in its surface dynamics. The poem is especially compelling for its aesthetically sustained framing of the assignment of women's and men's roles in culture and, more specifically, in its externalization of male presence. In the poem Bogan achieves the inverse of the internalization of male values that a number of her critics decry, for her poem, however critical it may be of women's accommodations to patriarchy, renders extraneous to women those forces that may appear to circumscribe them:

> Women have no wilderness in them,
> They are provident instead,

Content in the tight hot cell of their hearts
To eat dusty bread.

They do not see cattle cropping red winter grass,
They do not hear
Snow water going down under culverts
Shallow and clear.

They wait, when they should turn to journeys,
They stiffen, when they should bend.
They use against themselves that benevolence
To which no man is friend.

They cannot think of so many crops to a field
Or of clean wood cleft by an axe.
Their love is an eager meaninglessness
Too tense, or too lax.

They hear in every whisper that speaks to them
A shout and a cry.
As like as not, when they take life over their door-sills
They should let it go by.

(*BE* 19)

"Women"—with its distancing use of the third person *they* and its seemingly accusatory parallels—has been cited as symptomatic of Bogan's adoption of masculinist assumptions that denigrate women. Pope finds the poem "devastating"[15] and argues that Bogan puts forward "the utterly bleak proposition that women are by gender unable to love, to move, to be free, that it is neither landscapes, partners, nor roles, but women's very selves that are ultimately 'the body of this death.'"[16] Elizabeth Frank asserts that the poem depicts women as "by nature tinged with defective wills" and cites the poem for "its obvious *envy* of maleness."[17] Taking a different approach altogether, Ronald Giles argues for an ironic reading, noting that Bogan's speaker, "appearing to itemize attitudes and attributes of womanhood, . . . actually reveals, in a tone of cynical understatement, the masculine imperfections from which men take such perverse satisfaction."[18] The speaker shows women to be "provident, sentient, benevolent," and "more sophisticated" than men.[19] Giles's reversals call attention to the poem's ostensible values ("If men *can* think of 'so many crops to a field' or of 'clean wood cleft by an axe,' so what?").[20] While Giles's essay opposes critics who present the poem as representative of Bogan's sympathies with patriarchy, his reading strains the poem's rhetoric and largely overlooks its genuine denunciation of women's acculturated status.

Although the poet's position as a woman problematizes our reception of the poem, her gender does not annul her actual uneasiness with women's status. Bogan is indeed an accomplished ironist, yet objections to women's strategies of accommodation to male privilege inform the poem and provide for much of its critical power. In the logic of the poem, women occupy an internal realm, men an external one. Ironically, as the poem's assumed "other," men, like women, "have no wilderness in them," for their activities revolve around rural domestication; they tend cattle, plant fields, chop wood. Although superficially representing her central gender as "content in the tight hot cell of their hearts," Bogan portrays women's discontent and restlessness: "they hear in every whisper that speaks to them / A shout and a cry." The object of their love (presumably men) cannot satisfy, for men's love is the origin of "an eager meaninglessness." The references to maleness (Is men's love the "dusty bread" women eat in their cells? Are men simply to be "let . . . go by?") are specific only in regard to men's avoidance of generosity: Women "use against themselves that benevolence / To which *no man* is friend" (emphasis mine). The one quality explicitly repudiated by men, benevolence, is placed in critical focus. Characteristically, Bogan indicts cultural ideology that leads to women's self-sacrifice. She repudiates traditional cultural expectations of women's kindnesses— kindnesses that women have traditionally been discouraged from practicing toward themselves. If employed against selfhood, such negative benevolence allows any "life" to enter, even that which should be rejected. At the conclusion, men are expelled from the site of the poem, presumably as "life" that should be "let go . . . by."

"Women," then, is an overt critique of women's acculturated behavior and an implicit critique of men's. In particular, Bogan explores the physical and psychological constriction of women and the externalization of men in regard to women's intimate concerns. Even should men physically enter women's realm rather than be "let . . . go by," in the poem they are experienced by women as a curious absence. Justifiably, the poem is one of Bogan's best known, for it challenges the reader's desires for harmony and affiliation. Its conceptual separations are conceived in the dramatic terms that generate Bogan's characteristic oppositional posture in her early career.

It would seem evident that Bogan's reliance on a conception of difference between women and men and on acts of extraction and separation reflect a means of psychological survival that she learned early in life. In recent years much of Bogan's private history has come to light through the

1973 publication of a volume of her letters, edited by Ruth Limmer; through Limmer's 1980 "mosaic" of Bogan's autobiographical materials; and through Elizabeth Frank's 1985 biography. Critics have reconstructed Bogan's life in ways that illuminate her personal and professional conflicts and, most particularly, Frank has memorably revealed Bogan's embattled progression toward maturity.[21] Bogan's own accounts suggest that, with difficulty, she labored to separate herself from overwhelming and capricious others. *Body of This Death* draws from and reflects upon Bogan's multiple experiences of rupture. She had survived not only the childhood trauma of temporary abandonments by her mother but she had undergone rapid metamorphoses within four years of early adulthood as a wife, mother, and widow.

When *Body of This Death* appeared, most reviewers greeted it with some puzzlement as a whole, even as they praised individual poems. With the exception of Llewellyn Jones they did not examine the ways in which oppositional circumstances are framed in Bogan's poetry. Mark Van Doren began his review with a characteristic qualm: "It is impossible to say what these twenty-seven poems are, and it would be difficult to say what they are like."[22] More insightfully, Jones describes Bogan's first book as "the poetry of struggle against—shall we say, circumstance? Not circumstance in the gross sense of the word, but against all that stifles, diverts, and disarms life in its original intention; against the pettiness that haunts the footsteps of love, especially against the limitations, imposed and self-imposed, on women; and, at the same time a cry for something positive, for something compelling."[23] What Bogan had sounded was a note of unqualified resistance to a cultural role of negative symbiosis between men and women and a cultural denial of women's positions of dissent. In related terms, her defiance of coercion, particularly that of the group, was a theme that she emphasized early and late:

> It was borne in upon me, all during my adolescence, that I was a "Mick," no matter what my other faults or virtues might be. It took me a long time to take this fact easily, and to understand the situation which gave rise to the minor persecutions I endured at the hands of supposedly educated and humane people.—I came from the white-collar class and it was difficult to erase the dangerous tendencies—the impulse to "rise" and respect "nice people"—of this class. These tendencies I have wrung out of my spiritual constitution with a great deal of success, I am proud to say.[24]

Repeatedly, Bogan was able to create a critical separation between her resolutely high ideals for poetry and the reality of her own productions, enabling her to look sternly upon her less-successful poems. Her 1941 letter to John Hall Wheelock regarding the proof sheets of *Poems and New Poems* reveals her own sense of standards—and her vision of her younger self, the woman who wrote *Body of This Death*:

> I find it easy to send back this proof quickly; there is nothing controversial in the choices.—I don't think, however, that we can keep "A Letter." There is something wrong with it; I can't say just what. Something sentimental or unfinished or mawkish. Whatever it is, I don't like it. So please let's take it out.—I don't like "Love me because I am lost," either. Don't you think we might dispense with that, as well?
>
> It isn't that I'm turning on my early self. But the girl of 23 and 24, who wrote most of these early poems, was so seldom mawkish, that I want her not to be mawkish at all.[25]

Her demand for the integrity of the poem, and for a complex poetic voice, remained uncompromising throughout her career. Although unwilling to describe Bogan as an empowering voice, Paula Bennett's own focus on separation actually suggests the impetus toward critical division that Bogan's poetry, drawn as it is from her experience, enacts. Bennett argues that "Just as the child learns to differentiate himself or herself from the mother by saying no, so the woman artist must say her no to draw the necessary limits around herself and her life that will protect her integrity and allow her to reconcile herself with her gift."[26]

We might consider in this context an early poem from *Body of This Death* in which a woman must be extracted from a ruling conception— indeed, extracted in a way that must have been piercingly familiar to the young Bogan. In "The Romantic" a man would "name" a woman "chaste," denying her bodily desire, that trope in Bogan's work for life energy. Ascribing a nullifying purity to a woman and attempting "to fix and name her," the romantic proves adept only at denial. Finally, the woman eludes his plans and entirely escapes figuration in the present. At best, her past may be described (and surely someone will be glad to describe "what she was"), but neither her present nor her future may be narrated. Both resist interpretation:

> In her obedient breast, all that ran free
> You thought to bind, like echoes in a shell.
> At the year's end, you promised, it would be
> The unstrung leaves, and not her heart, that fell.
>
> So the year broke and vanished on the screen
> You cast about her; summer went to haws.

> This, by your leave, is what she should have been,—
> Another man will tell you what she was.

(BE 12)

Although a traditional romantic conception would limit her, the woman ultimately refuses to be divorced from her own bodily experience. The regularity of the poem's three rhyming quatrains is juxtaposed against the situation's irony, for the poem effects a final disappearance of structural constraints as the woman escapes the romantic's predictions. By reflecting division between the romantic man and the object of his desire, Bogan alludes to the absence of true intimacy between women and men in the conventions of romantic love.

"The Frightened Man," first published in February 1923 in *Measure*, depicts a man's fear of his desires in a way that again suggests absence, a profound separation between women and men, and a cultural denial of the power of "changed women," represented by "the rich mouth" in this early poem. The frightened man is fearful of sexually appetitive and emotionally changeable women, and seeks control by avoiding "the rich mouth":

> In fear of the rich mouth
> I kissed the thin,—
> Even that was a trap
> To snare me in.
>
> . . . . . .
>
> O, forget her praise,
> And how I sought her
> Through a hazardous maze
> By shafted water.

(BE 6)

Here the mouth serves as a disturbing synecdoche; the female mouth appears to devour and deceive, and yet the mouth soon enough draws praise and pursuit. Although the frightened man claims that the woman has been changed, he himself is transformed. It is his perception of the woman rather than the woman herself that alters. While the frightened man believes that "the thin mouth" has "become strong / And proves relentless," he has eagerly pursued the woman through a landscape that mirrors his conflicted desires: "a hazardous maze / By shafted water." Through the poem's three swift quatrains and its emphatic stresses we are confronted with the isolated consciousness of a central speaker who views his experience as both dangerous and, ironically, elusive.

The implicit laceration of "shafted water" in "The Frightened Man" is duplicated in Bogan's many descriptions of romantic love. The draft of an unpublished poem, "Beginning of an Unpopular Song" suggests her sense of romantic love's daunting, and often destructive, hold upon personality: "Stopping wild love is (believe me) like stopping fever in the veins."[27] In another unpublished poem, "Letter to Mrs. Q's Sister," Bogan situates her speaker as an outsider to an affair who finds monotony in the pangs of romantic love, particularly in illicit romance: "Adulterer's letters, unfortunately, are always the same."[28] In her early twenties she was already critical of melodramatic immersion in romantic love among her contemporaries. "My Voice Not Being Proud" refutes a reigning attitude among some of her contemporaries of hyperemotionality regarding romance. As Elizabeth Frank points out, the poem may be Bogan's response to Edna St. Vincent Millay's pose in "The Shroud" from *Renascence* (1917).[29] In Bogan's poem the poetic voice that shouts its sensitivity to love and loss is repulsed. Her speaker exposes romantic pretension. Desire, as Bogan well knew, would inevitably end, at least in death. There was no use in protesting desire's strength and choosing death before life. Pointedly, this is the work of a young woman who is calling upon her poetic elders—and her contemporaries—to abandon romantic and rhetorical excess for a greater truth of feeling.

If she rejected what she considered the melodramatic posturing of some of her contemporaries at the time that she wrote *Body of This Death*, Bogan nevertheless understood the impetus to abandon identity for a dream of unity through romantic love, as "Men Loved Wholly Beyond Wisdom" suggests:

> Heart, so subtle now, and trembling,
> What a marvel to be wise,
> To love never in this manner!
> To be quiet in the fern
> Like a thing gone dead and still,
> Listening to the prisoned cricket
> Shake its terrible, dissembling
> Music in the granite hill.

> (*BE* 16)

The observer's fate is a passive quiescence. To repress love, to fail to understand it, to remain simply blameless, as such, presents no solution. Finally, to abjure desire without understanding would mean to be obsessed in yet another way, for one is then left as a witness, perpetually fearing desire, "Like a thing gone dead and still, / Listening to the prisoned cricket" of one's own heart. Bogan refused to ignore the lure of romantic love; those who did so might be anaesthetized before any power larger than self-interest and a counterfeit "wisdom." To fail to comprehend passion is simply to mimic paralysis, as both "Men Loved Wholly Beyond Wisdom" and an unpublished poem, "Hell," even more broadly make clear. In the latter poem, "The dead sit still, done with the heart. / Their laughter lifts their jaws apart; / They sit and watch the stage forever." Those without an understanding of romantic love are, as such, "Able to grin, but not to weep."[30] Such empty and wry passivity, Bogan suggests, cannot serve as a useful counter to romantic obsession. Instead, a difficult understanding must emerge, and a healthy resistance to any form of violation must be fostered.

In a number of other poems Bogan delineates the complexities of psychological separation and merging. She believed in the capacity to engage in passionate love and yet balked at the extremes of romantic infatuation that denied the independence of one or both partners and that fed on a specious self-denial on the part of women. Clearly, she knew that in her investigations of romantic love she resisted a major and compelling mythology of her time. Her lyrics of romantic love, however, do not simply track disillusion. Nor was her position absolutist. She saw in the first experiences of romantic love the tentative possibility for the early practices of a new alchemy of sorts; if one could begin to comprehend romantic love and progress beyond its limited boundaries to discover independence and fidelity (the latter, the most elusive of virtues for this poet) perhaps one might undergo a necessary initiation into maturity.

Bogan's statement in a self-interview suggests that her own earliest romantic searches were marred by psychological mirroring. To the question "By what means did you seek love," she answers:

> I had no means. I was stupid, an exile in myself, sunk in a deep self-mirroring, self-effacing dream. I presented a still surface to the appearances around me, like a glass, stiffened into a polish capable of reflection by the same insane cohesion that keeps the particles of stone firmly within the stone. (*JAR* 56)

This suspicion of romantic fusion continued to preoccupy her after *Body of This Death*, as "Man Alone," first published in the *New Yorker* in November 1934, suggests. A man who would "read" his being through feminine presence must inevitably find himself estranged. And the speaker remains a "stranger" to the narcissist who seeks his reflection through her. She must insist upon her own psychological separation from him:

> It is yourself you seek
> In a long rage,

Scanning through light and darkness
Mirrors, the page,

. . . .

The glass does not dissolve;
Like walls the mirrors stand;
The printed page gives back
Words by another hand.

And your infatuate eye
Meets not itself below:
Strangers lie in your arms
As I lie now.

(*BE* 75)

The final imperfect rhyme underscores the failed correspondence between these lovers, and the poem's title emphasizes that although the speaker of the poem is now in the man's arms, the man himself remains ultimately alone in his narcissism.

The woman whose presence erupts most emphatically at the conclusion of "Man Alone" was anticipated in the earlier poem, "Fifteenth Farewell." The speaker of "Fifteenth Farewell" in *Body of This Death* discovers her lover's emotional intangibility. His baffling solitude is the missing center that she attempts to address:

Your thought, beyond my touch, was tilted air
Ringed with as many borders as the wind.
How could I judge you gentle or unkind
When all bright flying space was in your care?

(*BE* 24)

The speaker has been emotionally distanced from her lover throughout their relationship, and yet she has denied this failure in intimacy. Her farewell amounts to an anguished attempt—her fifteenth—to understand the absence about which the relationship centered. The form of the Italian sonnet is doubled, as if the speaker must multiply her efforts to deliver herself from a fruitless obsession.

The metaphor of mirroring that appears here is explored in a number of Bogan's poems and proves significant. Without clear psychological boundaries we simply reflect others, and a crippling symbiosis occurs. "Portrait" presents Bogan's awareness of a quest for emotional maturity. The woman in the poem need not "be a glass, where to foresee / Another's ravage" (*BE* 11). No longer reflecting her lover's desire, she is "possessed by time." If the latter phrase suggests erotic devaluation and sudden mortality, it also may initiate another possibility: now the woman may more fully experience the mutable world and her own presence within it. Similarly, in "The Crows" a passionate older woman "hears the crows' cry" and gains knowledge. As the crows jeer "Over what yields not, and what yields" (*BE* 17), the mature woman learns that, while culturally assigned to youth, desire may overcome age itself.

A spirit of profound criticism animates many of Bogan's poems. Indeed, for some readers during her lifetime she was more widely known as a critic than as a poet. Writing to Morton D. Zabel, Bogan jokingly reiterated her critical creed: "I write my criticism, what there is of it, out of my innate feeling for form, sincerity, music, truth, beauty, etc., etc., and my innate distaste for nincompoopery, dopishness, chaos, murk and balderdash."[31] The fine, and often witty, analytical discernment that she focused upon the poetry of her contemporaries clarifies as well the relationships that her own poems investigate. Externalizing an alien value structure rather than absorbing it, Bogan is not a comfortable figure, appropriated easily into any critical view. The challenge of her work emerges in part from a stylistic austerity that represents separation as a necessary resistance.

Within poems that are addressed most pointedly to women, stern lessons in perception are granted one woman to another. Such lessons rely on images and acts of separation. "The Crossed Apple" was first published seven years after *Body of This Death*, testifying to the endurance of the motif of rupture in Bogan's work. In what seems to be a rewriting of *Snow White*, a presumably older woman presents a young woman with a divided apple: a choice between peaceful nurturance, "Meadow Milk," or the sufferings of consuming obsession, "Sweet Burning":

> I've come to give you fruit from out my orchard,
> Of wide report.
> I have trees there that bear me many apples
> Of every sort:
> Clear, streakèd; red and russet; green and golden;
> Sour and sweet.
> This apple's from a tree yet unbeholden,
> Where two kinds meet,—
>
> So that this side is red without a dapple,
> And this side's hue
> Is clear and snowy. It's a lovely apple.
> It is for you.

Within are five black pips as big as peas,
As you will find,
Potent to breed you five great apple trees
Of varying kind:

To breed you wood for fire, leaves for shade,
Apples for sauce.
Oh, this is a good apple for a maid,
It is a cross,

Fine on the finer, so the flesh is tight,
And grained like silk.
Sweet Burning gave the red side, and the white
Is Meadow Milk.

Eat it; and you will taste more than the fruit:
The blossom, too,
The sun, the air, the darkness at the root,
The rain, the dew,

The earth we came to, and the time we flee,
The fire and the breast.
I claim the white part, maiden, that's for me.
You take the rest.

                                        (*BE* 45–46)

While embodying experience that is segregated into extremes ("this side is red without a dapple, / And this side's hue / Is clear and snowy"), the crossed apple serves as the focus of an ironic schooling. The older woman's offering may prove, if the maiden will interpret her gift correctly, a lesson in self-interest. Whether a wizened Eve or a revisionary witch, this speaker does not betray herself or engage in self-delusion. And the maiden whom she addresses might refuse extremes of experience or—if she prefers—she might seek to "claim" the apple half that "is clear and snowy" for herself. In "The Crossed Apple" Bogan presents not only a criticism of needless suffering mandated within romantic love (the "sweet burning" that gives the poem its one intentionally melodramatic note), but she extends an invitation to experience serenity. Questioning romantic illusion and self-sacrifice in love, she presents a "crossed" gift to women: a poetry of profound criticism rather than of simple affirmation. She reveals the obsessive nature of "sweet burning" but holds out the possibility of release, the "meadow milk" of the divided fruit.

In "The Crossed Apple" the action of the witchlike persona—her claim to tranquility and her refusal to embrace the destructive (however seductive) experience of "sweet burning"—counterbalances the excesses of culture that define women as inevitably benevolent and accepting. Defeating "self-mirroring," Bogan reveals her impatience with the multiple impediments to expression in *Body of This Death*. Her first book dramatizes her capacity to overturn conventional pieties as her speakers announce their will to separate themselves from any controlling force, whether a cultural repudiation of women's artistic capacities or the restraints of conventional romantic love. "To act *on* life; to be a *subject*, not an object":[32] this was her recurrent desire. We might recall Adrienne Rich's observation that Bogan's poetry proves "a graph of the struggle to commit a female sensibility, in all its aspects, to language." Rich further observes, "We who inherit that struggle have much to learn from her."[33] Bogan's poetry of separation offers an invigorating challenge to her readers. Her aesthetics too often have remained obscured by readers who seek directness and affirmation. As a consequence, Bogan has become a puzzling Athena of modern American poetry. But instead of casting her poetics as a "paradigm" of oppression and self-hate, we might do well to remember Bogan's repudiation of suffering in "The Crossed Apple" and the example that she dramatizes of positive, if rather wickedly proffered, self-concern:

> I claim the white part, maiden, that's for me.
> You take the rest.

2

Repression and Secrecy:
Dark Summer

In "*turning something away, and keeping it at a distance, from the conscious*"—the act that Sigmund Freud defined as "*the essence of repression*"[1]—Louise Bogan discovered one of her most complex subjects. As a woman in a culture that inhibited female voice and female memory, as a childhood witness to violence who had herself repressed the origin of her temporary blindness, and as a poet who believed that her most achieved poetry arose from unconscious forces, she was uniquely positioned to explore repression.

Although separation and violence in overt or subterranean form are often figured in her early work, in *Dark Summer* (1929) Bogan most fully investigates repression and secrecy. The summer referred to in her title is dark not only because of an inauspicious emotional climate but because some elements of this "season" have been withdrawn from consciousness. Elizabeth Frank speculates that the entire collection's many references to darkness represent "latency, concealment, and imminence, for whatever lies at a remove from will and control. Above all, darkness signifies the deepest layer of the unconscious, where hidden instinct gathers force and prepares to obliterate the powers of both reason and resistance by which the 'vulgar upper consciousness' makes its claim to mastery."[2] In her second book we might read Bogan as a poet actively engaged in tracing the contours of repression, the "dark summer" of the psyche.

In her title poem, written at Yaddo in 1926, summer is characterized by what is withheld or denied, suggesting the dynamics of repression:

> Under the thunder-dark, the cicadas resound.
> The storm in the sky mounts, but is not yet heard.
> The shaft and the flash wait, but are not yet found.

The apples that hang and swell for the late comer,
The simple spell, the rite not for our word,
The kisses not for our mouths,—light the dark summer.

(BE 41)

Her characteristic anxiety about composition ("The simple spell, the rite not for our word") marks the poem, as do indications of psychic and erotic deprivation that nevertheless drive the speaker to desire creative speech. "The shaft and the flash" allude not only to the expected storm's lightning but to the shaft of the pen and the flash of inspiration. The tercets embody force sustained without discharge, the initial strong caesurae culminating with the final caesura marked by both a comma and a dash. Each possibility of release is anticipated and yet withheld.

As we shall see, Bogan's title poem in small compass reflects her attempt to study repression as it must finally "light the dark summer"; through her knowledge of the dynamics of repression she would not only discover new subject matter for herself but determine one source of her power as a poet.

In the six years between the publication of *Body of This Death* and *Dark Summer*, Bogan had firmly established herself in the literary circles of New York City, securing friendships, for instance, with Edmund Wilson and Rolfe Humphries. In 1923 she met the poet and novelist Raymond Holden, who would become her second husband, and in the spring of 1924 she wrote her first review for the *New Republic*, at Wilson's urging, and performed as acting editor of the *Measure*, continuing on the editorial board for three years. In July of the following year, 1925, she married Holden, a marriage that, perhaps because of its passion, apparently reawakened in new form her childhood fears of abandonment and betrayal.

In *Dark Summer* she explores repression by creating poems in which psychic materials appear to be pressing at consciousness. One of her best-known journal statements, written on 21 September 1961, suggests that such material is the poem's source, for "the repressed becomes the poem":

The poet represses the outright narrative of his life. He absorbs it, along with life itself. The repressed becomes the poem. Actually, I have written down my experience in the closest detail. But the rough and vulgar facts are not there. (*JAR* 72)

The absorbed experience emerges in new form; repression amounts to poetic source. As Hélène Cixous provocatively remarks: "[P]oetry involves gaining strength through the unconscious and . . . the unconscious, that other limitless country, is the place where the repressed manage to survive:

women. . . ."[3] Bogan's compressed forms and contextual omissions allow her to allude to the unconscious and, I would suggest, to the cultural placement of women. For Bogan, then, peculiar strength may be found in images of repression and, in similar terms, of concealment.

To her own question in a self-interview, "How do you think that your apperceptions, your perceptions can be reproduced?," Bogan replied, "By chance, by indirection, by reference" (*JAR* 57). She believed that poetry was a seemingly inexhaustible medium for resonant suggestiveness and as such it came closest to expressing the most profound and complex elements of experience. Her description of the nature of modern poetry proves illuminating in this context: "The line of modern poetry is a persistent—though sometimes devious and diverted—line toward new structure, new largeness, and new power; directed by an undeviating search, not for an absolute and all-embracing aesthetic 'machine,' but for a commodious and flexible carrier of complicated thought and sensibility."[4] Assuming that she has not excluded her own work from "the line of modern poetry," Bogan's description outlines the function of meaning within her poetry. However sheared of explanatory material about personal incidents, the poems in their reference become "commodious and flexible."

It is significant that in her prose memoirs and autobiographical fiction Bogan favors those images and scenes that resist ascriptions of totalizing meaning. An account in the short story "Dove and Serpent" about her early memory of decorations at a neighbor's home proves illustrative:

> Her son's sword hung on the wall of the sitting room; a doll in a paper skirt, that held string, hung beside it. I used to look at these two objects for long unbroken periods; they possessed some significance that I could not pry out of them with my eyes or my mind. The doll and the sword were so pretty and so unexpected. The sword had a tasseled belt twisted around its handle. The doll's little feet under the paper skirt, the string appearing from the middle of a rosette in its sash, its bisque head and real hair and hard small mouth open in a smile—this was a problem I could not solve. As I remember my bewilderment, my judgment even now can do nothing to make things clear. The child has nothing to which it can compare the situation. And everything that then was strange is even stranger in retrospect. (*JAR* 4–5)

Bogan suggests that disjunctive images are to be looked at for "long unbroken periods"; such images do not relinquish accessible meaning. We cannot force an "equation," for they present an unelucidated disunion. Such memories would seem to offer profound implications about sexual and gender ascriptions. Writing of this and other memories in "Dove and Serpent," she noted, "It is such memories, compounded of bewilderment and ignorance and fear, that we must always keep in our hearts. We can never forget them because we cannot understand them, and because they are of no use" (*JAR* 8). She duplicates such an effect of extreme and unelucidated juxtaposition within her poetry.

In *Dark Summer*, poems bare of motivating circumstance mimic the compressed dynamics of the unconscious and resist singular readings that objectify experience. Much of the poems' uncanny power derives from the way they intimate repressed materials. In this context, by alluding to "repression" I have in mind Bogan's investigation of how "the repressed becomes the poem," or how material usually unavailable to consciousness may be insinuated through the poem. Indeed, Bogan suggests the volatility of repression in a way that underscores Freud's conceptions. As Freud proposed:

> [R]epression does not hinder the instinctual representative from continuing to exist in the unconscious, from organizing itself further, putting out derivatives and establishing connections. Repression in fact interferes only with the relation of the instinctual representative to *one* psychical system, namely, to that of the conscious.[5]

Bogan would embody in language the repressive situation, and she would simultaneously move toward a qualified form of expression. Her omission or compression of biographical material may be seen in some measure as a consequence of her aspirations for her own poetry, illuminated in an uncollected poem written, most likely, in 1932. The poem clarifies the "dialogue" that she conducted with herself and makes explicit her search for authority within implosive containment and through withheld context, characteristics that she allied to unconscious activities. The poem that refuses to "confess" or "expose" may enhance its capacity to intimate the mysteries of the unconscious:

> I thought to make
> The smallest possible compass for loveliness
> For safety's sake;
>
> To cheat the skill
> Of any who might well measure or covet it
> Against my will.
>
> "They have big eyes;
> This, if it be but a little seed-point of brightness,
> They will not prize."

But you said "No;
It is the little thing that the marksman looks for
With his long, spliced bow.

The arrow takes
(With luck) a line into the target's centre,
Holds there, and shakes.

If the archer be clever
The landscape about him is scattered with tiniest marks
Speared neatly forever."

What shall I do?
It cannot be small, so that any casual arrow
May rive it in two.

Beyond all size,
Secret and huge, I shall mount it over the world,
Before the bolt flies.[6]

Bogan's speaker wishes to evade appropriation by critics or rivals: "To cheat the skill / Of any who might well measure or covet it / Against my will." Yet she fears that the "little seed-point of brightness"—the compressed poem—may be too easily possessed, for a second voice proposes that the critic/reader prefers "smallness" in order to capture "neatly forever" the moment in time to which the poem alludes, and thus to possess the poem and master its meaning. Finally, the principal speaker resolves her conflict by rejecting limiting measure and by uniting oppositions. The poem must be "Beyond all size / secret and huge." She would master paradox, making the poem impervious to its critics as a creation of both privacy and magnitude; indeed, privacy, the secretive, would seem to be, for her, an essential element of "magnitude," thereby granting the poem its greatest resonance. Further describing Bogan's ambition, Elder Olson contemplates how the omission of context in her poems may contribute to their subterranean force: "[T]he setting, the whole circumstantial periphery of action, is shown with great vividness, the sharp images compel our imagination and our belief, the reticent and yet pregnant method of representation forces us to wonder and conjecture; and a part of the inexhaustible fascination of these poems surely resides in the fact that no conjecture fully satisfies us."[7] Indeed, Bogan's work is, to a large extent, *about* the very experience of repression and concealment. Surely her fascination with omitted context is not simply a symptom of her anxiety as a poet. More fully, the covert assumes new meaning and complex power; the enigmatic and the repressed dilate her lyrics.

Two poems may be especially interesting for their exploration of covert psychological states. "Winter Swan" and "The Cupola" are both nearly bare of incident but marked as "containers" of repression. Interior experience in "Winter Swan" melds physical and psychic energies:

> It is a hollow garden, under the cloud;
> Beneath the heel a hollow earth is turned;
> Within the mind the live blood shouts aloud;
> Under the breast the willing blood is burned,
> Shut with the fire passed and the fire returned.
> But speak, you proud!
> Where lies the leaf-caught world once thought abiding,
> Now but a dry disarray and artifice?
> Here, to the ripple cut by the cold, drifts this
> Bird, the long throat bent back, and the eyes in hiding.
>
> (*BE* 29)

Through a complex rhyme scheme, repetition of words (*hollow, blood, under, fire*), and syntactic parallels, she creates a seemingly inviolable stylistic. All lines but the penultimate are end-stopped, the penultimate line's enjambment pulling us toward the image of the bird, just as the bird itself is compelled forward within circumscribed limits. Positional words (*under*, occurring twice, and *beneath* and *within*) depict the scene as covert and internalized. Within the mind, "the live blood shouts aloud" and within the heart "the willing blood is burned." In an arena in which Robert Frost's inner and outer weathers are irreconcilable, she creates an image of the swan as a hybrid answer to her question concerning the disappearance of summer and the emergence of winter's "disorder and artifice." The "hollow garden" and "hollow earth" seem to be an echoing unreality, as if representing a landscape of the unconscious. If we would will meaning upon this uninscribed landscape ("But speak, you proud!"), we may find that the swan is itself a silent cipher of repression: "the long throat bent back, and the eyes in hiding." Bogan's swan must drift, resisting appropriation, a sign of recalcitrance to customary meaning and event. Although a conventional symbol of beauty, particularly poetic and feminine beauty, here the swan serves as a figure for repression. Soundless, its eyes hidden, it signals repression through its very pose. Even if we are to return to "the live blood" and "the willing blood" of the poem, we find that mind and body have at core this frozen figure.

Bogan focuses again on repression in "The Cupola," imagining a space from which "the repressed becomes the poem" as a rounded, abandoned dome that suggests female space. A secret place, "shuttered" and "abandoned," the cupola has at its center a mirror reflecting natural processes throughout the seasons:

> A mirror hangs on the wall of the draughty cupola.
> Within the depths of glass mix the oak and the beech leaf,
> Once held to the boughs' shape, but now to the shape of the wind.
>
> Someone has hung the mirror here for no reason,
> In the shuttered room, an eye for the drifted leaves,
> For the oak leaf, the beech, a handsbreadth of darkest reflection.
>
> Someone has thought alike of the bough and the wind
> And struck their shape to the wall. Each in its season
> Spills negligent death throughout the abandoned chamber.
>
> (*BE* 34)

The poem is spare in its use of rhyme, and more relaxed in its employment of assonance and alliteration than are many of Bogan's poems of this period. The long lines and repeated prepositional phrases further relax the poem. The second stanza, however, creates a shift in meaning even while repeating the essentials of the first stanza: a mirror has been placed in the cupola. But the syntactical change and the additions, so quietly effected, are critical: *someone* has placed the mirror here "for no reason," and the mirror itself is now an "eye," linked metaphorically to the body. Yet like Bogan's swan, the mirror reflects what would seem to be not only seasonal change but a psychic reality beyond reason. Significantly, the agent of this transforming act—the unnamed "someone" who has placed the mirror in the cupola—is absent and unknown. This "someone" has put the mirror in a position to intimate repression: the unconscious condenses time, and the poem refracts a knowledge of human and seasonal violence.

The final stanza opens by reiterating the former presence of this unnamed person: "Someone has thought alike of the bough and the wind." As in "A Tale" this "someone" reduces difference, indeed reduces categories of being: "The bough and the wind" are not differentiated, and the result of this placement of the mirror, this seemingly unmotivated act, "spills negligent death throughout the abandoned chamber." The adjectives *negligent* and *abandoned* would seem, in this minimalist, controlled scene, to be cast back as descriptives of the human agent, the unknown, unidentified "someone."

At the poem's conclusion, as Charles O. Hartmann suggests, we experience a heightening of feeling:

> Bogan's words conform to the syntactical grid native to English, though the analogy of a rectangular screen hardly conveys the complexity of that system. Her words also belong to lines. The reader barely notices the separate existence of the first six lines, so directly do they match the syntax. Though they generate attention, they do not shift its focus. But in the last stanza she tilts the sentence in relation to the lines. The effect startles us; and in the context of the whole poem, we interpret the surprise as a sudden passion in the speaking voice.[8]

From what would initially serve as a spare description of interior space, we are finally left with a perceptual "tilt" in which the speaker chooses newly to understand her plight as a mortal subject split between unconscious impulse and conscious knowledge. The mirror as "eye" is for Bogan similar to her poetry, for the mirror/eye provides a different form of ordering for us, a doubling of scene, as the visible and the invisible, and what is living and what is not, are equally considered: "Someone has thought alike of the bough and the wind." For all the blunting of difference in the drafty room, the poem's stark images are magnified as interior symbols. The mirror of "darkest reflection"—the poem, born from repressed material—may bring to consciousness the fact of mortality and violence. On one level, the cupola as mysterious enclosed space serves as a spatial representation of the unconscious.

We might recall that Sandra Gilbert and Susan Gubar in their important early study *The Madwoman in the Attic* observe that "anxieties about space" have been prevalent in literature by women writers in both the nineteenth and the twentieth centuries: "[F]rom Emily Dickinson's haunted chambers to H.D.'s tightly shut sea-shells and Sylvia Plath's grave-caves, imagery of entrapment expresses the woman writer's sense that she has been dispossessed precisely because she is so thoroughly possessed—and possessed in every sense of the word."[9] The particular possession that Bogan chooses to reflect on in her poems is rooted in her desire both to delineate her intuitions about the unconscious and progressively to confront and express inchoate conflicts, tentatively to name and at least temporarily to "possess" confining space rather than simply to be possessed by it. She would trace a shape that might allow access to latent psychic processes.

Our understanding of Bogan's investigation of the unconscious in "The

Cupola" may be deepened if we consider her essay, "Detective Novels" (1944). Bogan was attracted to qualities in the detective novel that are vitally present in her poetry. Her nearly obsessive focus on secrecy and repression is evident in her description of Poe's detective stories:

> The detective novel splits off from the surrounding anarchy of form. And within its closed universe Poe further limits its locale by inventing the convention of the locked room. The detective now has completely rejected his bloodhound role. He becomes the scientist "coordinating indices," the artist-priest astounding the world at large as well as his rather stupid human foil. The crime becomes as isolated from life as a chemical experiment.[10]

In this instance, Bogan's prose presents a transformed and condensed description of the abandoned and shuttered cupola of her poem, a cupola that is as curiously isolated as the scene of a crime, "the locked room," in a detective novel. And if we take "The Cupola" as a coded detective plot of sorts, her reiteration of death in the cupola turns uncanny. The unconscious is a repository in this poetry for repressed memories of violence; pointedly, the arranger in "The Cupola" has "*struck* . . . images to the wall" (emphasis mine) reflecting disorder and the casual violence of "negligent death." Writing elsewhere of her birthplace and its cupola (a connection indicating that the poem may derive from unconscious associations with childhood) Bogan notes, "The house has *such* a cupola and eaves made of gingerbread, and in the picture's foreground my mother is holding me, an infant of six months, of extremely simple appearance, in her arms."[11] The cupola is integral to the remembered scene, and, as we shall learn by reading Bogan's autobiographical prose, the pictured child will become the victim of an unstable and violent home. If we take into account her memories of her early past, Bogan's description of the detective novel is particularly suggestive of her own childhood and the repressed events that are inscribed within her poetry. As she wrote of the detective novel, "The victim is always there, whether the sign of a brutal sacrifice or a more human oblation."[12] She reserved unusual praise for the detective novel as a genre that may contain "secrets of what we are and shall be."[13] In "The Cupola" the very fact of violence would seem to drum at the walls of this seemingly quiet poem, nearly a still life that intimates the very power of repression.

Significantly, in her journal Bogan reminisces at length about the orderly household of a woman with whom the Bogan family for a time boarded. In Mrs. Gardner's house all necessities and conveniences were in proper and pleasing order. As a seven-year-old who could not yet read, Bogan discovered that "the house was [her] book." The rooms in the house

duplicated two of her own aesthetic principles: those of careful economy
and formal design. And yet Mrs. Gardner's house surely cannot serve as a
final representation of Bogan's fullest relationship to interior space. Tellingly,
when thinking of the room of Mrs. Gardner's daughter, Bogan imagines
herself as an outsider: "It is at the door, looking in, that I always see myself, in memory" (*JAR* 17). She views herself as a threshold figure counting
and cataloging details, and the well-appointed room, while it unmistakably
provides a vision of harmony and security, cannot symbolically contain the
tension of her mature poetic. A room such as that of "The Cupola" reveals
another dimension of experience that includes elements of repression, and
the "poem as room" stands as a representation of a place in which disorder
and order conflict. In her journal of 1959 she considers the house in which
she first learned to read in a manner that may clarify her developed sense of
interior space as haunted by opposing forces, those of efficiency and order,
and those of a malignant disorder in which the past casts a shadow on all
present activities:

> The dream is always the same. I go back to the house as I now am. I put into
> it my chairs, my pictures, but most of all my books. Sometimes the entire
> second floor has become a library, filled with books I have never seen in
> reality but which I have close knowledge of in the dream. I rearrange the
> house from top to bottom: new curtains at the windows, new pictures on the
> walls. But somehow the old rooms are still there—like shadows, seeping
> through. Indestructible. Fixed. (*JAR* 30)

It is this "double vision" of the past saturating current attempts to reorder
space that she examines most fully in *Dark Summer*.

Reception of *Dark Summer* was generally favorable, although Bogan
faced criticism for her handling of long poems from both Morton D. Zabel
and Yvor Winters. In his review, Zabel characterizes her poems as "rare
and beautiful" but gently faults Bogan for her handling of structure. And
although he praises "Old Countryside" and "Simple Autumnal," what he
finds in these intricate poems is, in his rather deflating terms, "a subtle
interest in homely realism."[14] Like most critics, Winters admired Bogan's
mastery of the lyric. Nevertheless, he discovered "certain technical limitations" in her long poems, and he found her work more complex in style and
emotion than in "idea." He otherwise reserves high praise for Bogan, linking
her to the metaphysical poets: "It would take only a turn, a flicker, to trans-
form her into a major poet; it is conceivable that the flicker may be taking
place as I write, that it may even have occurred in her book, *à mon insu*."[15]

In general, Bogan was pleased by these and other reviews for the distinguished comparisons they made between her work and that of earlier poets, particularly the seventeenth-century poets whose concentrated images and highly charged comparisons she partially emulated. And certainly her reviewers could not be harder than she herself was on her work. Yet when writing to her publisher John Hall Wheelock, she singled out Winters's review, revealing her penchant to review the reviewer. Written shortly after the review appeared, Bogan's letter to Wheelock points out that Winters's own thoughts readily were inflamed by emotion, even of a (comically) violent cast:

> He is *such* a serious, learned, conscientious boy, so passionately for style and dignity in writing, and for ethics and humanism in life. . . . I thought the review so serious and intelligent that perhaps it will make people flee in horror from this modern *soi-distant* combination of Campion, Jonson, and Dryden! Yvor loves argument; he cannot write a review without dragging in special pleading for the restitution of metaphysical birthright to modern American writers. I have seen him, at a very gay dinner party, when all the other guests were making themselves wreaths out of the centerpieces, almost come to fisticuffs with Arthur Ficke over Gerard Manley Hopkins![16]

If Winters praised her work in certain terms, he nonetheless failed to consider the way that thought in her poetry emanated from emotion itself; certainly, although she primarily valued emotion in poetry, her work was not as simple in "idea" as he asserted. In a review of Bogan's later poetry, Marianne Moore would more insightfully note, "[T]here is fire in the brazier—the thinker in the poet."[17] And in her study of Bogan, Jacqueline Ridgeway observes, "It is the intellectual analysis of feeling that makes for intricacy in many of Bogan's poems."[18]

It would seem that early critical focus on Bogan's exactitude and technique may have obscured recognition of her complex subject matter. In nearly obsessive form in *Dark Summer*, Bogan explores the repression of grief and its ultimate, although qualified, expression. As Gloria Bowles has observed, "A concordance to Bogan's poetry would produce 'grief,' that old word, one with rich and deep literary association, as one of the recurring motifs" of *Dark Summer*.[19] Paul Ramsey refers to the way grief "persistently and profoundly underdwells her poems."[20] Bogan's poems of grief acknowledge repressed energies that inhibit the discharge of accumulated tensions. If conventional wisdom since Freud tells us that grief must eventually be expressed and, as such, released, Bogan explores the peculiarly mixed conditions inhibiting grief's release. In particular, she creates poems as holding spaces, or pressurized psychic containers, in which grief initially is denied full expression. Writing decades later of her experience as it influenced her aesthetic choices, Bogan notes: "What mattered got into the poems. Except for one or two *stories*, which I may be able to tell, it is all there. With the self-pity left out" (*JAR* 172). Her own experience is compressed to reveal its essentials and to widen applicability and reference, making the poems, paradoxically, both "huge" and "secret" through their renewing mystery.

The sensation of repressed materials straining upon awareness may account in part for some of the intensity of *Dark Summer*. We might read it as a book in which release is frustrated and speakers are suffused with sorrow. Julia Kristeva's exploration of grief in *Black Sun* extends our observations, for like Kristeva, Bogan finds in mourning a psychic "place" to be investigated. In *Black Sun* Kristeva discusses depressed persons' keen sense of their predicament, including their experience of "metaphysical lucidity," saying they are supremely aware of "the meaninglessness of Being."[21] Kristeva argues that loss and division are necessary to speech: "Speaking beings, from the ability to endure in time up to their enthusiastic, learned, or simply amusing constructions, demand a break, a renunciation, an unease at their foundations."[22] The work of art, then, offers a sphere in which new linguistic play intersects with "the unnamed agitations of an omnipotent self that ordinary social and linguistic usage always leave somewhat orphaned and plunged into mourning."[23] Such "agitations" predominate in Bogan's *Dark Summer*. Mourning is effectively suppressed even while speakers achieve lucidity about what Kristeva calls "the meaninglessness of Being." Kristeva's argument is echoed in Bogan's own journal description of depression: "That winter of her depression, a small round camera eye opened and shut in her memory and suddenly a scene would be disclosed with terrific clarity: she reassembled, in a flash, a scene complete to the kind of shadows on the ground and the kind of weather in the sky" (*JAR* 97). Depression for Bogan at least partially implied moments of supreme "lucidity" as images and scenes from the past were disclosed for her in high relief. Indeed, in *Dark Summer*'s "Late," Bogan gestures toward unconstructed meaning, a stark reflection upon her environment:

> The cormorant still screams
> Over cave and promontory.
> Stony wings and bleak glory
> Battle in your dreams.
> Now sullen and deranged,
> Not simply, as a child,

> You look upon the earth
> And find it harrowed and wild.
> Now, only to mock
> At the sterile cliff laid bare,
> At the cold pure sky unchanged,
> You look upon the rock,
> You look upon the air.

> (*BE* 39)

The bare final lines depict a consciousness that equates and reduces manifold phenomena, for this is a consciousness stayed by withheld grief.

In a more complex examination of repression, "the burned, restless but abiding leaf" (reminiscent of the leaves in "The Cupola") serves for the speaker's self-perception. A taut-skinned fullness, a psychic engorgement, delays expression in "Simple Autumnal":

> The cone, the curving fruit should fall away,
> The vine stem crumble, ripe grain know its sheaf.
> Bonded to time, fires should have done, be brief,
> But, serfs to sleep, they glitter and they stay.
>
> Because not last nor first, grief in its prime
> Wakes in the day, and hears of life's intent.
> Sorrow would break the seal stamped over time
> And set the baskets where the bough is bent.
>
> Full season's come, yet filled trees keep the sky
> And never scent the ground where they must lie.

> (*BE* 40)

The images of "Simple Autumnal" project the withheld sensations of repression: "the tearless eyes and heart, forbidden grief." Contained and denied expression, painful emotion does not diminish. Although the time for expression appears overdue, no means of release is available, and any expression undergoes a "delay." As Frank observes, the poem is "a perverse defiance of that process Freud called 'grief-work,' whereby painful memories must be reexperienced, and relinquished."[24] In the sonnet's final stanza, Bogan departs from a four-line stanza to a couplet with exact rhyme as emotions undergo condensation: "Full season's come, yet filled trees keep the sky / And never scent the ground where they must lie." Such unreleased grief petrifies, and as a result sensory experience is diminished.

In other poems, the withheld expression of grief may tentatively suggest psychic wealth. In "If We Take All Gold" repressed materials do not dissolve but at best may be "hidden" as secret riches, "the repressed that becomes the poem." The sterility of "Late," its enactment of a descent into meaningless and narrowed context, is here contradicted by Bogan's conception of "sorrow's gold":

> If we take all gold
> And put all gold by,
> Lay by the treasure
> In the shelved earth's crevice,
> Under, under the deepest,
> Store sorrow's gold:
> That which we thought precious
> And guarded even in sleep
> Under the miserly pillow,
> If it be hid away
> Lost under dark heaped ground,
> Then shall we have peace,
> Sorrow's gold being taken
> From out the clean house,
> From the rifled coffers put by.

(*BE* 30)

Allowing sorrow to "be hid away" may make possible at least an appearance of serenity. Yet Bogan's ambiguous syntax renders the poem an open exploration rather than a closed argument. Only tentatively does "sorrow's gold" offer the conclusion that we may take up the repressed from the "coffers" that may be "rifled." A greater syntactic and conceptual emphasis is placed upon a new burial, a further investment in repression. And although the poem refers to a burial in earth, its metaphors figure the earth as cupboardlike, "the *shelved* earth's crevice" (emphasis mine), linking nature to Bogan's frequent imagery of enclosed space.

In "Didactic Piece," written in 1925, Bogan addresses a course that may release grief's expression. The title alone suggests that she was bent on instruction of sorts—not simply self-instruction, but instruction of her readers on the course that her own thinking was taking. The title makes clear, as well, Bogan's degree of self-consciousness. By unabashedly calling attention to the poem as a teaching device, she might hope to deflate criticism of her abstract plan for dealing with emotional pain. Yet the poem, for all its didacticism, remains intensely personal; it seems derived from her intense desire to understand more deeply the early events in her life. The poem reveals some of her discoveries at this date about her psyche, discoveries that she felt could not be peculiar to her own condition. She "teaches" us that initiating events that led to present misfortune must once again be confronted and "lived-through." But she also addresses in the poem the psyche's resistance to this process. Obsession, after all, defeats the perception of time, resulting in psychic paralysis in which one simply repeats past patterns of reaction. The images of the tree, the apple, and the heart (among her most frequent) reappear in "Didactic Piece," yet nature, to which her speaker had turned for comfort after loss in the earlier poem "Knowledge," does not ultimately comfort in this context. Her speaker must secure her emancipation from the psychological effects of the past by reexamining and reexperiencing the most threatening primary incidents that had been denied.

The poem begins with an eye "unacquitted." This unpardoned gaze is figured as "the hard bud," a trope for repression as withheld energy:

> The limit already traced must be returned to and visited,
> Touched, spanned, proclaimed, else the heart's time be all:
> The small beaten disk, under the bent shell of stars,
> Beside rocks in the road, dust, and the nameless herbs,
> Beside rocks in the water, marked by the heeled-back
>   current,
> Seeing, in all autumns, the felled leaf betray the wind.
> . . . .
> Let the allegiance go; the tree and the hard bud seed
>   themselves.
> The end is set, whether it be sought or relinquished.
> We wait, we hear, facing the mask without eyes,
> Grief without grief, facing the eyeless music.
>
> (*BE* 42)

Although the speaker is brought to the point of tears by music, she nevertheless checks her impulses. If she is pulled toward the expression of grief by music's power, she is soon repulsed from expression by her awareness of music's artifice. The "mimic despair" of another's art cannot dissolve her own grief; another's artifice may not fully release her own disordered feeling. At this point we might hear an echo of the earlier poem, "My Voice Not Being Proud." Once again Bogan rejects the possibility of being a profligate of her own emotions. If the speaker of "Didactic Piece" would prefer to contemplate only beginnings, imagining "the hard bud seen under the lid, not the scorned leaf and the apple," even the air conspires to reveal mortality and, consequently, cause for disquiet. The poem's final stanza, then, does not facilely follow through on what seems to be the Freudian lesson of the second stanza. For now she dramatizes the very difficulty of coming to terms with the essential mysteries of the personal past, and she ends the poem with an image of unreleased grief, of a "mask without eyes," a monstrous obscuring form drawing the poem toward closure. If the self is to be "the felled leaf [that must] betray the wind," she intimates a power that brutally shapes fate. To "betray the wind" is to disclose and identify the source of sorrow, as wind is frequently suggestive of an invisible but omnipresent and coercive force in this poetry. "The wind still carries you, but one day you will carry it," she told one of her students,[25] suggesting in cryptic terms her own desire for progress toward psychic and creative strength. Ultimately, "Didactic Poem" posits both the necessity and the difficulty of achieving psychic renewal. This renewal goes beyond "the heart's time," the time of the passions as they are fossilized by early violence. She must "return" to explore "the limit," the pattern of the past, within which her own psychic obsessions were forged. Here we see Bogan working out steely equations: she makes clear that only through the most courageous investigation of the psyche as it is imprinted by early events can repression be understood and expression be freed, and yet she closes the poem by dramatizing the enormous challenges such an act poses.

We might again note Freud's description of *"the essence of repression"* as *"turning something away, and keeping it at a distance, from the conscious."* Repeatedly, Bogan examines this "turning . . . away" through imagery of, or direct statements about, sight. We should note that she defined her childhood with particular force when referring to her vision. Hers was the "candid yet fierce intensity of a child's gaze, that knew all the tricks of sight" (*JAR* 23). Her interest in vision derives in some measure from one of her earliest and most baffling experiences: the psychological blinding that she believed came about through the severe repression of an incident most likely involving her mother. During early childhood she was blind for two days. Of her temporary loss of sight Bogan recalls in her journal:

> The secret family angers and secret disruptions passed over my head, it must have been for a year or so. But for two days, I went blind. I remember my sight coming back, by seeing the flat forked light at the gas flame, in its etched glass shade, suddenly appearing beside the bureau. What had I seen? I shall never know. (*JAR* 26)

Concealment was accompanied by rage and disorder: "the secret family angers and secret disruptions." And precisely because of her awareness of its corrosiveness when concealment dominates family life, Bogan views secrecy (as she does repression, allied so closely, for her, to secrecy) with fascination. Having experienced a brief period of blindness and unable to recall the triggering event, she endows her poems with an enhanced awareness of both visible and invisible forces. Her connections between the experience of loss and visual experience are registered and elaborated upon so often in her work as to prove paradigmatic. We might recall that in "Winter Swan" the bird's eyes are hidden, and the summer itself is presented as if it were somehow spatially concealed, as if it were put out of place, out of sight, momentarily: "Where lies the leaf-caught world, once thought abiding. . . ." In "The Cupola" the mirror is figured as an "eye" reflecting a small but significant space. In the rampant fire of "Feuer-Nacht" an eye is "shuttered," and later in the poem "The eye in its lair / Quivers for sight" (*BE* 36), as if vision must be characterized as covert and menaced. The faculty of sight preoccupied her, as her letters and her poems make clear. In a letter to Robert Phelps, Bogan noted, "sometimes it seems . . . that the aesthetically experienced object is less like a lover than like a long-lost child. Do you remember what Hopkins said: that when we look *hard* at an object, it looks back *hard* at us!"[26] Her aesthetic internalizes the long-lost— implicitly that which is secret and unseen—just as "the long-lost child," her earliest remembered self, would preoccupy her in later poems.

The disappearance of sight, sight overwhelmed and sight extinguished, pervades a number of her more important poems, linking the issue of repression with obsessive concealment. As we have observed, confrontation often occurs as a visual moment in which a figure gazes upon an unknown other, as in "A Tale," "where something dreadful and another / *Look* quietly upon each other" (emphasis mine) (*BE* 3). Bogan's poetry enacts extreme confrontations and intimates in complex ways the workings of the unconscious which, in Jacques Lacan's terms, "is neither being, nor nonbeing, but the unrealized."[27] As Lacan asserts, the unconscious would seem to be predicated upon "the need to disappear that seems to be in some sense inherent in it—everything that, for a moment, appears in its slit seems to be destined by a sort of pre-emption, to close up again upon itself, as Freud himself used this metaphor, to vanish, to disappear."[28] Similarly, Bogan's poems resist conventions of reading and would seem to track "disappearance" itself.

"Division" in *Dark Summer* appears to be a commentary on Bogan's brief loss of sight during childhood, for the shadow that grows through "long days and changing weather" is emblematic of her repression of the event that led to her temporary blindness: "The burden of the seen / Is clasped against the eye." The shadow is itself a "burden" that duplicates the weight of repressed materials. Like the indelible trauma of the past, the shadow remains "woven in changeless leaves," as the repressed survives in the unconscious:

> Replica, turned to yourself
> Upon thinnest color and air—
> Woven in changeless leaves
> The burden of the seen
> Is clasped against the eye,
> Though assailed and undone is the green
> Upon the wall and the sky:
> Time and the tree stand there.

(*BE* 32)

Key words in the poem are repeated (*shadow* appears three times in seven lines, and *single* occurs at the ends of lines five and six). In so emphatically duplicating word choice the poem seems to absorb itself, its directional cues (*up, out, upon*) pointing toward the uneffaced memory trace. Bogan's curious use of the words *assailed* and *undone* connects seasonal change tentatively with sexual violation. The poet as the transformed Daphne in the image of the tree ("assailed and undone is the green") stands as a mute witness, disabled by having earlier repressed awareness of an offending figure. If we read the tree as the transformed Daphne, we may detect Bogan's depiction of a psyche captured by early events that are outwardly unexpressed yet ever-present in the unconscious. By delineating the shadow of unconscious materials, Bogan signifies the complex embedding of psychic materials as it is effected by sight.

In "The Mark" a shadow and hidden objects—here, apples—similarly serve to emblematize repression:

> Loosed only when, at noon and night,
> The body is the shadow's prison.
> The pivot swings into the light;
> The center left, the shadow risen
> To range out into time's long treason.
>
> Stand pinned to sight, while now, unbidden,
> The apple loosens, not at call,
> Falls to the field, and lies there hidden,—
> Another and another fall
> And lie there hidden, in spite of all

> The diagram of whirling shade,
> The visible, that thinks to spin
> Forever webs that time has made
> Though momently time wears them thin
> And all at length are gathered in.
>
> (*BE* 38)

In this rather involved conceit in which Bogan's affinity to the seventeenth-century metaphysical poets is pronounced, the shadow again becomes a figure for repression. Sight is tantalized in a manner that we may associate with the uncanny, described by one critic as "an effect caused by a sidelong look, something seen out of the corner of the eye, off to the side (and even 'off-side,' in the sense that inadmissible, repressed or suppressed material is frequently implicated in it)."[29] The conceit's intricate juxtapositions and correspondences had been attractive to Bogan since her introduction to the metaphysical poets in the 1920s, for she felt that the conceit represented an advanced level of understanding: an emotional and intellectual function that is wedded to complex figuration. In Samuel Johnson's famous description of the metaphysical poets' practice ("the most heterogeneous ideas are yoked by violence together") we may note some of the characteristics of her own practice at this time, for her images are placed in extreme juxtaposition. The poem accommodates the secretive and the uncanny through opposed images and introduces an enlarging mystery: "[P]oetry must deal with that self which man has not made, but has been presented with; with that mystery (by no means a totally absurd one) by which he finds himself surrounded. It is these gifts that the poet must spend his life confronting, describing, and trying to interpret" (*JAR* 67).

The central figure of "The Mark" is unable to evade his shadow—the effects of repressed materials, the initiating trauma of the past. The shadow, "marking no epoch but its own," points to Bogan's sense of a "psychic time," the time of the unconscious as events of the seemingly buried past coexist with present moments in an unconscious epoch. The poem's protagonist must "stand pinned to sight," as if the faculty of sight were paralyzing. The apples, hidden after falling in the grass, serve to make tangible the processes of psychic concealment and repression. In "Dark Summer," we might recall, "apples . . . hang and swell for the late comer" (*BE* 41). In "Simple Autumnal" we see that "filled trees keep the sky / And never scent the ground where they must lie" (*BE* 40).

In "The Mark" Bogan imagines ripe and fallen apples that nevertheless defy sight and forgo possession, just as past trauma remains unavailable to consciousness but seemingly volatile within the unconscious. The "fruits" in this poetry, and by extension the poems themselves as "fruits" of the poet's labors, often are positioned to symbolize concealment.

In other poems a suggestion of violence tests the limits of vision, as in the final stanza of "Old Countryside":

> Far back, we saw, in the stillest of the year,
> The scrawled vine shudder, and the rose-branch show
> Red to the thorns, and, sharp as sight can bear,
> The thin hound's body arched against the snow.
>
> (BE 52)

The stillness of this elemental scene in a poem dominated by austere monosyllables intimates not only repressed early memory, the "old countryside" of the unconscious, but suggests that repression threatens sight itself. Notably, the depiction is "sharp as sight can bear"; violence in nature mirrors psychological violence. The concluding image remains ambiguous, for the "arched" body might be in flight or, on the contrary, frozen in death.

It is important to note that when she wrote about women's poetry, Bogan focused on the metaphor of the lost jewel, a metaphor that suggests the resonance that concealed materials held for her: "It is a good thing for young women to bring to mind the fact that lost fragments of the work of certain women poets—of Emily Dickinson no less than of the Sappho quoted by Longinus as an example of 'the sublime'—are searched for less with the care and eagerness of the scholar looking for bits of shattered human art, than with the hungry eyes of the treasure hunter, looking for some lost grain of a destroyed jewel."[30] Whatever was lost, concealed, abandoned, or repressed would be the material of her own poetry. Characteristically, she figured the creative act as casting a privileged glow on acts of secrecy. Most important, finally, are "battles . . . fought in secret," as she asserted in a critical essay. Significant poetic expression cannot simply be released at will; the poet must struggle through a crisis "at all levels," particularly at the level of the first secrecies:

> No amount of heroic action, no adherence to noble beliefs can release poetic expression to order. The dialectical play of the mind or the aggressive action of the body affects its functioning not at all. Its battles are fought in secret and, perhaps, "are never lost or won." The certain method of stilling poetic talent is to substitute an outer battle for an inner one. A poet emerges from a spiritual crisis strengthened and refreshed only if he has been strong

enough to fight it through at all levels, and at the deepest first. One refusal to take up the gage thrown down by his own nature leaves the artist confused and maimed. And it is not one confrontation, but many, which must be dealt with and resolved. (*JAR* 116)

Bogan's distrust of emotional lability is contemplated further in "Tears in Sleep." In the poem a woman thwarts happiness by isolating herself with her grief. While over two decades later she would advise a correspondent who was mourning a family death to avoid any attempt to "suppress ... sorrow,"[31] she chose in "Tears in Sleep" to question a continued immersion in grief. Grief requires proper time, yet this speaker's expression of sorrow later plunges her into waking despair. The poem in its entirety reads:

> All night the cocks crew, under a moon like day,
> And I, in the cage of sleep, in a stranger's breast,
> Shed tears, like a task not to be put away—
> In the false light, false grief in my happy bed,
> A labor of tears, set against joy's undoing.
> I would not wake at your word, I had tears to say.
> I clung to the bars of the dream and they were said,
> And pain's derisive hand had given me rest
> From the night giving off flames, and the dark renewing.
>
> (*BE* 44)

Anxiously, the speaker wishes to dispel her grief, and yet she inhabits her dreams more fully than her lover's bed. Indeed, she is more connected with her ghostly lover, a dream stranger, than with the actual lover she sleeps beside. Her access to formerly repressed emotions is such that she is overwhelmed and does not experience actual release; she endures unrelieved suffering. "Long continued pain reduces one to the state of a blustering child," Bogan wrote in a journal entry, "or exacerbates one into an arrogant tyrant. Either 'I can't bear this; help me' (with tears); or 'I'm bearing this and don't you for a moment forget it'" (*JAR* 93). The unnatural night of "Tears in Sleep" reflects unnatural expression. Here grief is "false," "a labor of tears." The woman's repetitive suffering, what seems to be a willed insistence on clinging to past trauma, may be a means to avoid her present life, to achieve a reprieve from the even more painful forces of renewal. Characteristically, Bogan's speakers pause before undergoing what Freud calls "grief work," maintaining connection with a lost other or an earlier complex of feeling. Freud provides us with a view in *Mourning and Melancholia* that is particularly meaningful in this context:

> [P]eople never willingly abandon a libidinal position, not even, indeed, when a substitute is already beckoning to them. This opposition can be so intense that a turning away from reality takes place and a clinging to the object through the medium of a hallucinatory wishful psychosis.... [Reality's orders] are carried out bit by bit, at great expense of time and cathectic energy, and in the meantime the existence of the lost object is psychically prolonged.[32]

Bogan explores this opposition in which abandoning "a libidinal position" appears nearly impossible to the mourner; her speaker must weep for the past, but in doing so she neglects the present. Her mourners may seek to perpetuate their mourning, turning away from any present source of comfort as well as any living challenge.

A later poem, "Solitary Observation Brought Back from a Sojourn in Hell," provides evidence that Bogan's ambiguous responses to the process of grieving remained a vital theme throughout her life. Through her "sojourn in hell" in this late poem the speaker returns with a simple fact:

> At midnight tears
> Run into your ears.

> (*BE* 98)

This, Bogan's shortest poem, proves oddly comical and yet ultimately moving for its portrait of isolation. Just as the "observation" remains "solitary," so too does the speaker who weeps at midnight and later self-consciously notes the incongruity of her action. As if the products of grief were to reclaim and overwhelm the senses, weeping returns in a circuit to the body, frustrating release and perception. The couplet masquerades as light verse, briefer than its own title, yet its themes are drawn from among the deepest sources within Bogan's body of work.

Let us turn now to one of Bogan's most ambitious poems that charts the repression of grief and its ultimate, although qualified, expression. The placement of "Summer Wish" as the final poem of *Dark Summer* suggests a thematic progression from repression toward expression. Understandably, the poem gave Bogan considerable trouble in the making, for in some ways it is an oblique argument, composed despite Bogan's skepticism about the success of argument in lyric poetry. Later, in 1955, she wrote to May Sarton: "Of course, everything is material for poems—even the 'passive suffering' (sometimes) that Yeats deplored; but argument should be dramatized, as Yeats learned to dramatize.... It is impossible really to argue, in lyric poetry, because too many abstractions tend to creep in—and abstract ideas must get a coating of sensuous feeling before they become true poetic material; unless one is a born satirist."[33] While writing the poem in 1929, she observed, "For a time I despaired of it; now it has shape and sound, a climax or two and an ending that really excites me, all in the mind; one or two good intensive spurts will finish it, I trust."[34] The structure of the poem is particularly intricate. A first voice in the poem charts sources of trauma, attempting a catechism of former postures and strategies. A second voice marks orderly and benevolent seasonal change, serving as an oblique reply to the first voice's anguish and shame. The first voice proves abstract and yet dramatic; the second voice provides a lyric counterpoint of sensuous natural images of growth and change. While the form of counterpoint is borrowed from Yeats's *Shepherd and Goatherd*, a fact acknowledged in the poem's epigraph by a quotation, the problems that the poem charts have been treated in various experiments earlier in *Dark Summer*.

Somewhat like a contemporary Eve who realizes her nakedness, the first voice begins: "We call up the green to hide us." Spring appears as a summons to the sort of concealment that is familiar in so many of Bogan's poems of this period. Yet expression, the voice urges, must begin. The first voice would take up

> That tool we have used
> So that its haft is smooth; it knows the hand.
> Again we lift the wish to its expert uses, . . .
>
> (*BE* 53)

The wish ("It will be") is linked to the desire to compose both poem and self. Initially, the first voice remarks upon disguise and obstructed desire alone, "You cannot / Take yourself in" (*BE* 54). In this sphere of deadened feeling no composition would seem conceivable. What, then, could make expression occur? Not only knowledge of repression's source must be developed, she suggests, but one must also reexperience the origins of repression, a solution that we heard advanced in "Didactic Piece." Yet in "Summer Wish" Bogan is now unsparing in more directly searching out the sources of repression. To focus on the theme of repression is here to focus on the form of a search; she not only configures repression in *Dark Summer*, whether embodied as winter swan or shuttered cupola, but in "Summer Wish" she would trace the source of repression and discover a means to react to what seemed to her to be an initiating trauma. In "Summer Wish" the first voice presents one of her most explicit portraits of rage and familial violence—violence against a child.

Now must you listen again
To your own tears, shed as a child, hold the bruise
With your hand, and weep, fallen against the wall,
And beg, *Don't, don't*, while the pitiful rage goes on
That cannot stem itself?
Or, having come into woman's full estate,
Enter the rich field, walk between the bitter
Bowed grain, being compelled to serve,
To heed unchecked in the heart the reckless fury
That tears fresh day from day, destroys its traces,—
Now bear the blow too young?

                                                                    (*BE* 55)

Bogan delineates choices: to relive through memory the child's grief, a child who has "fallen against the wall"—or, as an adult woman, to "heed unchecked in the heart the reckless fury." Should one listen to the victimized child-self? Or should one obey the fury as internalized mother? Should one acknowledge the child—as victim? Or recognize the mother—as virago? The furious maternal may be internalized and, as such, "destroy its traces" and efface time, for the daughter's development hardly seems possible given the severity of such repression. We hear at this point an expression of anxiety, as if the speaker fears that she will once again *become* the victimized child. The alternatives are daunting; the other possibility allowed is that she become a woman amid "bitter / Bowed grain." Maturity here would seem to consist of self-negating service to others as a "bearer," a "reasonable" woman who serves others and yet evades her own psychic depths. We should note that both choices are united by violence: reliving the explicit violence experienced through memory or enduring the covert violence of repression. In either case, Bogan raises her questions and registers her ambivalence. To remember, after all, may mean to extract the maternal from unconscious denial and to submit the maternal to a horrible judgment; to internalize would mean to repress the child's anger and to enter "the rich field" in which mother and daughter may be complexly united in the psyche and yet together may be paralyzed by repression.

A cryptic description by the second voice serves as a comment on the first voice's fears:

In early April
At six o'clock the sun has not set; on the walls
It shines with scant light, pale, dilute, misplaced,
Light there's no use for. At overcast noon

The sun comes out in a flash, and is taken
Slowly back to the cloud.

(*BE* 55)

At this point in the poem it would seem that any hope for revelation and release from obsession is forestalled; even the natural world obscures its source of illumination. Nevertheless, the second voice announces that the work of creation has just begun in the fields, as it may, in turn, begin in the life of the agonized first speaker:

Fields are ploughed inward
From edge to center; furrows squaring off
Make dark lines far out in irregular fields,
On hills that are builded like great clouds that over them
Rise, to depart.
Furrow within furrow, square within a square,
Draw to the center where the team turns last.
Horses in half-ploughed fields
Make earth they walk upon a changing color.

(*BE* 58)

To this reborn measurement (the meter of planting suggesting the beginning of metrical plenitude) the first voice cries:

Speak out the wish like music, that has within it
The horn, the string, the drum pitched deep as grief.
Speak it like laughter, outward. O brave, O generous
Laughter that pours from the well of the body and draws
The bane that cheats the heart: aconite, nightshade,
Hellebore, hyssop, rue,—symbols and poisons
We drink, in fervor, thinking to gain thereby
Some difference, some distinction.

(*BE* 58)

The first voice then calls up a way of speaking and being that now integrates, in the poem's closing stanzas, the natural processes that the second voice had gently, yet unyieldingly, sought:

Speak it, as that man said, *as though the earth spoke*,
By the body of rock, shafts of heaved strata, separate,
Together.
    Though it be but for sleep at night,

> Speak out the wish.
> The vine we pitied is in leaf; the wild
> Honeysuckle blows by the granite.
>
> (*BE* 58–59)

"Separate, / Together": the image suggests the poise of oppositions that this poet records. This poise, paradoxically, makes a form of expression possible and evinces the desire of *Dark Summer*: a desire for at least qualified acceptance rather than denial of the ravages of past trauma or of betrayed and abandoned love.

Finally, the poem compels awareness of the dignity and voracity of the hawk as the poet's symbolic bird, allowing Bogan to cast a self-portrait of sorts in the poem's concluding image. Indeed, this partial self-portrait may most fully represent her ambivalence about both expression and repression:

> See now
> Open above the field, stilled in wing-stiffened flight,
> The stretched hawk fly.
>
> (*BE* 59)

In these few lines Bogan engages the poem's multiple tensions by appealing to our faculty of sight. To see is the key to release. Her speaker would no longer "turn away" in the Freudian sense of repression. As the first voice of "Summer Wish" cautions, "You have seen the ingrown look / Come at last upon a vision too strong / Ever to turn away" (*BE* 57). Repression must be countered by a refusal to swerve from the offending sight. The poet is, as the early "Medusa" suggests, fully aware of the dangers that a failure to see and to express metes out for the psyche. She recognizes as well the hazards of immediate and untimely expression: the falsity of a melodramatic lyric cry. Just as the "stretched hawk" is in movement, so, too, Bogan's poetry would represent a deepening sense of flux. What would appear to be the "stiffened" harness of formal poetry is a strategic posture that, like the hawk's, presents only an illusion of immobility.

Isolated and yet purposeful, Bogan suggests her ultimate stance through the hawk's flight. In meaningful terms, Harold Bloom has argued of Bogan's poetry: "As in Blake and Yeats, there is no transcendence of . . . strife . . . ; it is not resolved in the traditional consolations of religious belief, or in the expectation of any permanent abiding place for the human spirit."[35] From "Winter Swan," her first poem in *Dark Summer*, to her last poem in the book, concluding with a call to see a summer's hawk, the internalized force of repression is at last visualized as a figure of power. That Bogan has advanced in this collection from the image of the swan's eyes in hiding to the image of the hawk in open flight suggests her commitment to imagining degrees of psychic release.

What finally arises from Bogan's portraits of figures held in suspension before expressing grief? In some ways, her refusal to depict the immediate and full expression of contained psychological energy serves as a source of self-sufficiency. As "Summer Wish" suggests, her speakers consider a battery of responses, exploring self-dread, renunciation, and anger, but finally adopting a strategic balance, relinquishing the customary satisfactions of immediate self-release by refusing to present grief as a product to be consumed by readers. She would thwart the conventional association of women with superficial and ready emotions, for the emotions that she depicts are neither simple nor direct. At this point in her career, Bogan troubles our expectations of release in the lyric by writing of speakers positioned like the hawk in "Summer Wish," in "wing-stiffened flight," in strategic pursuit of some measured acceptance of crisis. Like the hawk, repression itself—should the poet refuse to gauge its strength and confront irrational impulses—is predatory, destroying its victim's perception of time and judgment. Yet poetry in its ungovernable suggestiveness may be one of the best instruments for embodying the effects of repression. The poem makes a space in language in which we may meet the irrational. The poem may allow us to trace the shape of the unconscious and to acknowledge the force of what may be withdrawn from awareness. That is, "the repressed becomes the poem." And her poems, in their refusal to elucidate their meanings, take on some of the power that she associated with the covert and the latent.

In her exploration of secrecy and repression, Bogan provides her readers with access to the experience of resistance. *Dark Summer* is perhaps her most puzzling book. Cheryl Walker, in fact, refers to it as "Bogan's maddest book."[36] Yet we might take Shoshana Felman's argument into consideration: "The more a text is 'mad'—the more, in other words, it resists interpretation—the more the specific modes of its resistance to reading constitute its 'subject' and its literariness. What literature recounts in each text is precisely *the specificity of its resistance to our reading*."[37] It is my sense that Bogan's poems provide a habitat in which the unelucidated and the unconscious may seemingly dwell. "Poetry is an activity of the spirit," Bogan argued, "its roots lie deep in the subconscious nature, and it withers if that nature is denied, neglected, or negated" (*JAR* 115). To acknowledge unconscious nature became increasingly urgent in Bogan's poetry. W. H. Auden addressed the issue of concealment in a review of Bogan's work that may prove provocative in this context: "[W]herever there is a gift, of whatever kind, there is also a guilty secret, a thorn in the flesh. . . ."[38] Her willingness to examine the effects of repression in *Dark Summer* proved preparation for her next book, *The Sleeping Fury*, as she moved from tracing the contours of repression to a recognition of that most beguiling figure, the mother.

3

Recognition of the Maternal:
The Sleeping Fury

In her early essay "The Springs of Poetry," Louise Bogan declares that the poet "should be blessed by the power to write behind clenched teeth, to subsidize his emotion by every trick and pretense so that it trickles out through other channels, if it be not essential to speech,—blessed too, by a spirit as loud as a houseful of alien voices, ever tortured and divided with itself."[1] That "divided house" is dramatized in the poems of separation in *Body of This Death,* in the poems of repression of *Dark Summer,* and, in another form, in her preoccupation with the primary experience of separation—the child's psychological separation from her mother—in *The Sleeping Fury.* Published eight years after *Dark Summer,* Bogan's third book approaches a new recognition of the mother. Traces of maternal presence can be found through elided references, acidic resistance to social force, and renewed emphasis on form making as it contains and neutralizes the disorder that is so clearly linked in Bogan's memory with her mother. Recognition itself, the unrepressed return of the gaze, is rendered most complexly in these poems.

Bogan's composition of *The Sleeping Fury* was accompanied by events of unusual intensity. In 1929 the house that she and Holden shared in Hillsdale, New York, was burned, destroying manuscripts of her poems and stories and many personal papers. "We are really quite well. Do not think us tragic figures," Bogan wrote to Harriet Monroe.[2] In 1931 she began reviewing poetry for the *New Yorker,* a venture that she was to continue for thirty-seven more years. But in the same year that she started work with the magazine she became a voluntary patient at the Neurological Institute for three months. "I refused to fall apart, so I have been taken apart, like a watch. I can truthfully say that the fires of hell can hold no terrors for me now."[3] Her psychic collapse was the first of three in her lifetime that required hospitalization, and she indicated repeatedly that the forces with which she struggled were derived from her childhood. In 1931 she explained her breakdown to Monroe:

> Several mechanisms have broken down and a strange new period has set in, in my heart and mind. I feel at once renewed and disinherited. Different people say different things. My doctor insists that I love; Robert Frost, whom we saw recently, recommends fear and hatred. But I have lost faith in universal panaceas—work is the one thing in which I really believe.[4]

Many years later Bogan wrote in illuminating terms of visiting one of the mill towns of her childhood, discovering intact the psychic atmosphere of her past that she believed precipitated her third breakdown in 1965 and that suggested to her the psychic battles that she had waged decades earlier, at the time she was writing her third book:

> —I felt the consuming, destroying, deforming passage of time; and the spectacle of my family's complete helplessness, in the face of their difficulties, swept over me. With no weapons against what was already becoming an overwhelming series of disasters—no insight, no self-knowledge, no inherited wisdom—I saw my father and mother (and my brother) as helpless victims of ignorance, wilfulness, and temperamental disabilities of a near-psychotic order—facing a period (after 1918) where even this small store of pathetic acquisitions would be swept away. The anguish which filled my spirit and mind may, perhaps, be said to have engendered (and reawakened) poisons long since dissipated, so that they gathered, like some noxious gas, at the v. center of my being. (*JAR* 47)

In 1933 she would travel to Europe on a Guggenheim Fellowship, but upon her return to New York the betrayal by Holden that she feared and that she perhaps exacerbated was confirmed.[5] He was deeply involved with another woman. In the same year Bogan suffered another breakdown.

While she was composing *The Sleeping Fury* Bogan was not only disturbed by her marriage, conditioned apparently by her early anticipation of betrayal in intimate relations, but she was also in some despair over critical neglect of her work. In 1936 she wrote to John Hall Wheelock: "The point is that I am the one poet in America, with a definite note, who is almost unknown."[6] It was in this frame of mind that Bogan opened *The Sleeping Fury* with an epigraph from Rilke. The epigraph from "Der Schauende" in *Das Buch der Bilder* reappeared in each of her subsequent books and encapsulates her struggle during the years in which she wrote her third collection:

> Wie ist das klein, womit wir ringen;
> was mit uns ringt, wie ist das gross . . .

Significantly, her fascination with Rilke's poetry, beginning in 1935, was based on his "terrific patience and power of *looking*."[7] She deeply admired his exploration of unconscious energies and his ability to endure: "Rilke was often exhausted, often afraid, often in flight, but he was capable of growth and solitude, a process and a state denied to the coward's or the delinquent's existence," she wrote in a review.[8]

With Rilke's spiritual example in mind, she organized *The Sleeping Fury* around a progression that charts fluctuations in emotional and psychological fortune. In a letter to Zabel, Bogan described the book:

> The S. F., is now in sections: four of them. It rises and falls, from despair, to exaltation, and back again: Bogan in cothurnus and Bogan in flat heels . . .
>
> Seriously, the poems shape up pretty well. The 1930-1933 period—despair, neurosis and alcoholism—is set off by itself, ending with "Hypocrite Swift." Then there is the period of further despair, edged in upon by the period of Beautiful Males (ending with "Man Alone"). Then the spiritual side begins, with a few rumbles from the sensual bassoons and the mystic fiddles. All ends on a note of calm: me and the landscape clasped in each other's arms.[9]

What she does not allude to is the book's broadened acknowledgment of the maternal as a creative body and as a figure for creative rupture itself. Bogan concentrates in three areas that redirect our attention to the maternal in subterranean form: she focuses on form-making power as it coexists with and appears in relation to the disorder and instability that she associated with her mother; she imaginatively occupies her mother's position by rejecting a social world that incites her suspicions; and she poses maternal creation against the "symbolic order" by recognizing fully the power of maternal energy.

As I am using the term in this context, "the maternal" refers not only to the poet's primary relationship with her actual mother, May Bogan, but to the ways in which her poetry disrupts the system of culturally assigned significance in language. Drawing on the work of Jacques Lacan and Nancy Chodorow, Margaret Homans presents a perspective on the maternal that bears upon the poetry of Louise Bogan. Homans speculates that women speak "two languages": that of the literal, derived from their early identification with their mothers, and that of the "figurative," the language of the

fathers, or "the symbolic order."[10] In Lacan's "symbolic order," the production of language is dependent on the absence of the mother; language
and culture must rely on an "absent referent." For women, however, as
Chodorow insists, the ties to the mother are not entirely dissolved through
an oedipal rupture. A sense of unity and identification with the mother
continues among women to a greater degree than among men. As Chodorow
argues, "As long as women mother, we can expect that a girl's preoedipal
period will be longer than that of a boy and that women, more than men,
will be more open to and preoccupied with those very relational issues that
go into mothering—feelings of primary identification, lack of separateness
or differentiation, ego and body-ego boundary issues and primary love not
under the sway of the reality principle."[11] For Homans, Chodorow's theory
bears directly on women's use of language. The two languages that Homans
postulates (the literal of the mother and the symbolic of the father) lead to
a rupture. The "presymbolic or literal language" that the daughter has learned
from the mother "with its lack of gaps between signifier and referent" may
not be entirely supplanted by the "father's language" but remains an inher-
itance that affects, in some measure, women's writing.[12]

Julia Kristeva's formulation of the maternal as it may threaten the symbolic order proves equally stimulating in this context. What Kristeva calls
"the immeasurable, unconfinable maternal body" is also the province of
the unconscious. An attempt to represent a state of preoedipal unity with
the mother would be "unutterable." Kristeva asks: "How can we verbalize
this prelinguistic, unrepresentable memory? Heraclitus' flux, Epicurus' at-
oms, the whirling dust of cabalic, Arab, and Indian mystics, and the stippled
drawings of psychedelics—all seem better metaphors than the theories of
Being, the logos, and its laws."[13] Referring to Plato's *Timaeus*, Kristeva
writes of the semiotic "chora" or "receptacle" that holds what is "unname-
able, improbable, hybrid, anterior to naming, to the One, to the father, and
consequently, maternally connoted to such an extent that it merits 'not even
the rank of syllable.'"[14] The traces in poetry of unintelligible vocalizations,
of "nonrecoverable syntactic ellisions,"[15] recall the child's first experiences
of the mother. Kristeva describes a "presymbolic and trans-symbolic relationship to the mother"—a relationship of which Bogan's poems bear traces
as she accomplishes what Kristeva describes as the compelling effect of
similar literary productions: "to signify what is untenable in the symbolic,
nominal, paternal function."[16] Bogan's ambiguous relation to the maternal
seems evidenced in the puzzling dualities that her poems present; rupture
in language would duplicate psychological rupture. As Homans argues, "If
the daughter's preoedipal closeness to her mother is accompanied by a
presymbolic language of presence, then when the daughter attempts to re-

create her symbiotic closeness with her mother, she is also attempting to recreate that presymbolic language."[17] Bogan's poetry, with its emphasis on form as it is aligned with the body and its figuration of the literal, and its "literalizations of figures,"[18] is profoundly marked by the poet's desire for the maternal. Her poems' ambiguous references and severe condensation, in turn, suggest her engagement with the language that Kristeva and other theorists link with the maternal.

Homans's description of women's "two languages" and Kristeva's emphasis on the maternal as it may menace the symbolic order prove useful in examining Bogan's poetry, particularly if we see the poet's work as influenced by her early psychological loss of a stable image of the mother. Significantly, Bogan presents herself as having been assaulted and separated in childhood from any sense of security. "I must have experienced violence from birth," she wrote in her autobiographical prose. "But I remember it, at first, as only bound up with *flight*. I was bundled up and carried away" (*JAR* 24). The very nature of such violence remains partially obscured as a secret that Bogan may not have even revealed to her psychiatrist, as a journal entry of the 1950s makes clear: "(But can I tell the whole truth? I never have, even to Dr. Wall. Is the emotional festering begun that far back?—Surely, farther back. . . . The early blows somehow *endured* . . .") (*JAR* 176).

While Bogan's poetry exhibits a peculiar mastery of the structures of the symbolic order, her mother's seemingly inexplicable nature provided a model for the exploration of repression and resistance that this poetry presents. Concealment, after all, seemed a tendency rooted in her mother's temperament, as depicted in Bogan's autobiographical short story "Dove and Serpent": "She could not go from one room to another without the intense purpose that must cover itself with stealth. She closed the door as though she had said goodbye to me and to truth and to the lamp she had cleaned that morning and to the table soon to be laid for supper, as though she faced some romantic subterfuge, some pleasant deceit" (*JAR* 6–7). Describing her mother at a window with her back turned, the poet recalls her mother's unavailability—and the persistently haunting quality of her elusive presence: "When she stood like this, she was puzzling to me; I knew nothing whatever about her; she was a stranger, I couldn't understand what she was" (*JAR* 5).

Apparently, Bogan's difficult relationship with her mother was a legacy of sorts, as her biographer suggests. Bogan's mother, Mary ("May") Helen Murphy Shields, was adopted by a woman named Shields and was educated at Mount Saint Mary Academy in Manchester, New Hampshire. She was given a refined upbringing and was known for her vivacity. May's own relationship to her adoptive mother (Frank points out that there is virtually no information available about her biological parents) was tempestuous. "During Louise Bogan's childhood," Frank notes, "her mother would often torment herself—especially on holidays—with feelings of guilt toward Mrs. Shields."[19] Her marriage to Daniel Bogan appeared to be impetuous and soon soured.

In a very early poem, first published in 1911 and inscribed with her youthful anxiety, Bogan endows nature with qualities that she associated with her mother's obsessive concealment. A speaker in the poem listens to the sea from her window as she lies in bed:

> I cannot sleep with all its whisperings,
>   I lie wide-eyed and hear the tide's swift rush
> Against the sand and sea-weed of the beach—
>   All through the night until the dawn it sings,
> Each ripple sighing—fading each in each—
>   And always, "Hush"—and always, always "Hush!"[20]

The sea's "whispering" disturbs consciousness and demands a private and unnatural allegiance. Like the maternal for Bogan, the sea calls for an implicit collusion. In illuminating terms, Frank reveals Bogan's early awareness of her mother's illicit affairs: "[T]ruth, for Louise, became charged with danger and doubleness. If Louise had told anyone what she knew about her mother, she too would have been guilty of betrayal, and would have targeted herself for her mother's rage. Yet, by keeping silent, she became an accomplice in the deception of her father."[21] Bogan's own descriptions of her early life focus on deprivation. The backyard lots of her childhood became signs for the emotional loss that she experienced: "The edge of things; the beaten dead end of nature, that fascinated me almost with a sexual fascination . . ." (*JAR* 20). Her accounts are typified by splits between natural and unnatural elements, order and disorder, presence and absence: "The incredibly ugly mill towns of my childhood, barely dissociated from the empty, haphazardly cultivated, half wild, half deserted countryside around them" (*JAR* 23).

Bogan's prose about her attempts to learn to read indicate the eruptive nature of her further entry into the symbolic. She did not learn to read easily, but once she did learn she relentlessly sought the order and security that reading offered. Of a childhood home, she writes: "Why do I remember this house as the happiest in my life? I was never really happy there. But now I realize that it was the house wherein I began to read, wholeheartedly and with pleasure" (*JAR* 30). She observes of a childhood book: "[I]ts contents were as delicious as food. They *were* food; they were *the begin-ning of a new life*. I had partially escaped. Nothing could really imprison me again. The door had opened, and I had begun to be free" (*JAR* 31, emphasis mine). In a telling metaphor she replaces her mother as source of nourishment, and as origin, with words themselves. Poetry offered a means of rebirth. As a fourteen-year-old writing poetry she discovered that "the life-saving process then began" (*JAR* 50).

Nevertheless, however much she may have resented her mother's ex-plosive temper and her unexplained absences from home, she did not choose to repudiate her mother. As Josephine Donovan has argued, women writers attain "emotional integrity" through their contact with the maternal. Draw-ing on Homans's work, Donovan observes that to succeed as writers, women "must learn to negotiate the 'no man's land' between two realms; they must learn two languages. If they remain in the preliterate world of silence, their production is absent, nonexistent, inaudible, and invisible. But if they lose touch with their mothers' gardens, they risk losing the emotional in-tegrity that is the source of artistic inspiration."[22] Despite the anxiety that she suffered as her mother's daughter, Bogan often stressed her identifica-tion with her mother. In the *Partisan Review* she described her gifts as "a remarkable excess of energy, on the maternal side of [her] family."[23] She wrote to Allen Tate, "I never cared for the Bogans. My mother, who was a Murphy and a Dublin O'Neil, adopted by a Shields, always held them in a certain amount of scorn; and all my talent comes from my mother's side."[24] In another letter she praised her mother's spirit:

> I made a visit to my own ancestral home, and am beginning to under-stand more and more what Yeats meant by "Paudeen," and why my mother was an admirable person, even if she nearly wrecked every ordinary life within sight.—She was against the penny-pinchers and logic-choppers; she loved beauty and threw everything away, and, what is most important, she was filled with the strongest vitality I have ever seen. —And how the "Paudeens" (from which the other side of my nature unfortunately stems!) hated and feared her![25]

Bogan's first book is dedicated to her mother and her daughter. As such, she inaugurates her career with notice of the maternal as herself both a daughter and a mother. A psychological continuity between mother and daughter is apparent in her descriptions of May Bogan: "A terrible, un-happy, lost, spoiled, bad-tempered child. A tender, contrite woman, with, somewhere in her blood, the rake's recklessness, the baffled artist's de-spair" (*JAR* 35). By framing her mother's behavior as the outgrowth of a "baffled artist's despair," Bogan forces an identification with her mother through assigning her an artistic temperament. And yet Bogan triumphs in this description by herself attaining stature as an actual and recognized artist, rather than a "baffled" one.

The pull between repudiation of and love for her mother is drawn in Bogan's narration of one of her mother's flights from their home in a journal entry of June 1959 that is worth quoting at length. After discussing her own enigmatic temporary loss of sight in early childhood, Bogan writes:

> But one (and final) scene of violence comes through. It is in lamplight, with strong shadows, and an open trunk is the center of it. The curved lid of the trunk is thrown back, and my mother is bending over the trunk, and packing things into it. She is crying and she screams. My father, somewhere in the shadows, groans as though he has been hurt. It is a scene of the utmost terror. And then my mother sweeps me into her arms, and carries me out of the room. She is fleeing; she is running away. Then I remember no more, until a quite different scene comes before my eyes. It is morning—earliest morning. My mother and I and another woman are in a wooden summerhouse on a lawn. The summerhouse is painted white and green, and it stands on a slight elevation, so that the cool pale light of a summer dawn pours around it on all sides. At some distance away the actual house stands, surrounded by ornamental shrubs which weep down upon the grass, or seem to crouch against it. The summerhouse itself casts a fanciful and distorted shadow. Then we are in the actual house, and I am putting my hands on a row of cold, smooth silk balls, which hang from the edge of a curtain. Then someone carries me upstairs. The woman goes ahead with a lamp. . . .
>
> Then I see her again. Now the late sun of early evening shoots long shadows like arrows, far beyond houses and trees: a low, late light, slanted across the field and river, throwing the shade of trees and thickets for a long distance before it, so that objects far distant from one another are bound together. I never truly feared her. Her tenderness was the other side of her terror. Perhaps, by this time, I had already become what I was for half my life: the semblance of a girl, in which some desires and illusions had been early assassinated: shot dead. (*JAR* 26–27)

In memory, Bogan casts her mother among "shadows like arrows" and images suggesting conflicting modes of division and unity. Light is "slanting . . . throwing the shade of trees and thickets for a long distance before it, so that objects far distant from one another are bound together." The mother in shadow would appear to be internalized, for if her daughter is unable to fear her, as Bogan asserts, it is in some measure because the mother as an internalized figure blocks the daughter's access to her own feelings. The child's "desires and illusions" are "early assassinated: shot dead." Mother and circumstance assassinate, but in the mixed language of Bogan's response to the maternal, pity and forgiveness are braced against more open complaint.

In her description Bogan images her own sense of split being through divisions between order and disorder and truth and deception. Two baffling and alien houses appear: a summerhouse that "casts a fanciful and distorted shadow" and an "actual house" in which the child contacts, momentarily, a perceived physical stability ("I am putting my hands on a row of cold, smooth silk balls, which hang from the edge of a curtain") only to be once again immediately swept up: "Someone carries me upstairs." Near this "actual house," as opposed to a summerhouse seemingly of illusion and resting on its "slight elevation," the appearance of foliage duplicates the child's undisguised physical reaction to her situation; the shrubs "weep down upon the grass, or seem to crouch against it."

In part, Bogan's prose account of her flight with her mother is a contemplation of the mother through a study of light. As John Muller resolves in a Lacanian reading, light in Bogan's poetry proves "a metonymy of the other; light begins a relationship by way of contiguity to the other's gaze, and the other's gaze, in turn, suffuses the world with desire, presenting to us the Other as desiring."[26] Arguing that light as an image dominates Bogan's poems and her journals, Muller links vision with "the mother's desire, passionate and erratic."[27] Bogan's identification with "her mother's desire" suggests the dangers of the gaze, making clear that "one source of vulnerability is the visual domain, namely, how the scopic field lures desire."[28]

Bogan's carefully controlled descriptions illuminate the ways in which simultaneously she would be drawn to embrace and to reject her mother. Nevertheless, it was May Bogan who offered the beginnings of artistic identity (however "baffled") and whose independent energy and air of mystery provided a model for Bogan's poetry in its dynamics of highly charged and secretive space. Both mother and poem would appear seductive and yet impossible to possess.

In Bogan's response to her mother she found, as well, the means of investigating cultural order. Her knowledge of her mother's distresses supported her awareness of the arid structure of many women's conventional lives. Her mother's desperation, the recognition of which apparently caused her daughter considerable distress, was symptomatic within a culture that denied women's desires. "Art Embroidery," a two-paragraph piece for the *New Republic* published in 1928, focuses on the spiritual emptiness that Bogan saw as prescribed for many women:

To push through this female crowd is difficult. These backs and arms
and sides have a terrific solidity. They are heavy—wider at the feet than at
the head. They have clean gloves, obstinate bright glances (a veil pulled
over the sagging lines that have been creased by animal pain, and by grief
more deep than the flesh can remember; over the dull eyes so used to door
and window, table, bed and chair, the curtain raised in the morning, the lamp
lit at night, the known faces pressed again and again into the eyes), slightly
perfumed bosoms, neat shoes. They can wait, three deep, shoulder to shoulder, at the counters under whose glass the cotton and silk lie pressed like
keepsakes. Tons of machinery, enough to crack them all to bits, rock behind
the walls, over the ceiling, under the floors.[29]

Such women are conjoined to find relief in triviality even as they are ob-
scurely threatened by man-made forces. Yet we should note that the bitterness of this account is not directed against women but against their cultural
situation, for confronting the women are both the confinements of domestic duties, registered here in terms of the women's limited environment,
and the intimidating presence of a hostile technology: "tons of machinery,
enough to crack them all to bits." The women are not only oppressed by
routine but by a technology that they have not been allowed to comprehend
and that apparently endangers them. More specifically, Bogan elsewhere
expressed what she felt was her own mother's sense of confinement within
a culture that threatened her desires, making palpable, at the same time, her
own awareness of women's cultural plight: "My father had his job, which
kept him in touch with reality; it was his life, always. My mother had nothing but her temperament, her fantasies, her despairs, her secrets, her sub-
terfuges" (*JAR* 48). Of the constricted possibilities for women like her
mother as they aged, Bogan writes:

In the youth of a handsome woman, two currents and two demands run
side by side in almost perfect accord: her own vanity's desire for praise and
love, and the delight in the praise and love so easily given her. When these
two currents lessen, a terrible loneliness and an hysterical dis-ease take their
place. For the energy once expended on delight and conquest now has nothing on which it can be dissipated; it is continually meeting small defeats and
rebuffs; it is like a river which has made a broad bed for itself, but now has
dwindled into a tiny stream that makes hardly any show among the wide
sweep of pebbles that show the boundaries of its former strength. (*JAR* 49)

It would seem clear that in her critical essays Bogan's description of
women's status emerges largely from her keen sense of cultural restriction,

that is, from circumstance rather than essence. While she did not view history as involving the perennial domination of women by men through all ages, she was deeply aware of the cultural restrictions on women of her time. She noted of women in general: "They are capable of originality and breadth of emotional and intellectual reference as soon as their background opens to any breadth and variety. They are often forced to waste their powers in an inadequate milieu, in social improvisation; to tack back and forth between revolt and conservatism."[30] An "inadequate milieu" seemed, to Bogan, nearly a definition of women's situation. Her ambivalence toward her own situation, including her wish to transcend gender altogether, was at times pronounced. Nevertheless, she continued to investigate the very nature of difference. In condensed form, Bogan's poems comment upon women's peculiar position in culture even more provocatively than does her prose.

To reach a fuller understanding of Bogan's involvement with the maternal, it is useful to return to her earliest poems about maternal presence. In "Medusa," first published in the *New Republic* in 1921, Bogan enacts a break from living being to deadening stasis, precisely rendering the moment of division. The poem is in five stanzas, four of them quatrains. The second stanza is composed of five lines, as if the stanzaic form must enlarge slightly to accommodate the Gorgon's ability suddenly to change conceptions of time and space. The repeated sibilants emphasize Medusa's threatening, snakelike power. With the poem's alternating line lengths, the first and third lines of quatrains often more than doubling in syllables the second and fourth lines, the poem mirrors the effect of foreshortening, contracting upon itself as the speaker in the poem experiences an abrupt halt in motion.

Initially, the woman who speaks is a threshold figure who sees the Medusa's head "through a door." The Gorgon herself would appear curiously without volition, suggesting that what may be viewed is her decapitated head, which will share the same fate as her victim, for her eyes, likewise, will be stiff and "bald," unable to turn from an offending sight. In his 1961 essay on Bogan, Roethke points out the connection between the speaker and the Medusa, noting that the Medusa is herself located in womblike maternal space, "the house in a cave of trees." Roethke was the first to suggest that the Medusa of Bogan's poems is "the anima, the Medusa, the man-in-the-woman, mother—her mother, possibly. . . ."[31] Medusa paralyzes beings who are then confined forever to her yard and, by extension, to the maternal. Immobilized, the speaker remains attached to her "creator" within "the great balanced day":

When the bare eyes were before me
And the hissing hair,
Held up at a window, seen through a door.
The stiff bald eyes, the serpents on the forehead
Formed in the air.

This is a dead scene forever now.
Nothing will ever stir.
The end will never brighten it more than this,
Nor the rain blur.

The water will always fall, and will not fall,
And the tipped bell make no sound.
The grass will always be growing for hay
Deep on the ground.

                                                                  (*BE* 4)

"Medusa" is marked by Bogan's central conflicts: a threateningly perme-able consciousness; ruptures between will and action; and ambivalence toward maternal power as the speaker is, in a sense, "shot dead." Beyond such conflict, the poem emerges, despite its ambiguities, as a paean to ma-ternal power even when that power is dislocated and cut from its source. As Karen Elias-Button has contended, the Medusa encloses "female cre-ative energies." Such a "Terrible Mother" proves a "metaphor for the sources of our own creative powers."[32] In "Medusa" Bogan creates a testament to the frightening power of the maternal and, in subterranean form, intimates her own identification with her mother, for Gorgon and speaker assume similarities through sight as the "stiff bald eyes" of Medusa are mirrored in those of the speaker. Ensnared in Medusa's gaze and duplicating the Gorgon's perceptions, the speaker must continually gaze ahead, her own eyes rigidified by staring. Finally, she is a "shadow" Medusa:

And I shall stand here like a shadow
Under the great balanced day,
My eyes on the yellow dust, that was lifting in the wind,
And does not drift away.

The poem's network of assonance and word repetitions (*bell, fall, shadow*) further emphasize mirroring, the effect of alliteration between lines allow-ing us to experience an aural identification, linking sound and semantics. And from the depth of the poem's ambiguity, the mother emerges as both a bonding and a blinding force. "What *did* happen—to her? I shall never know," Bogan writes of her mother in her autobiographical prose (*JAR* 36). In considering her psychological blinding during childhood, prompted by an event in some way linked to her mother, she duplicates such language: "What had I seen? I shall never know" (*JAR* 26). Loss of sight and loss of mother are, for Bogan, somehow combined effects, and both would seem to resist her understanding.

In her effort to represent the mystery of the maternal, a mystery that infiltrated numerous aspects of her experience and her poetry, Bogan portrays ruptures succeeded by fleeting moments of unity. "Betrothed," a poem detailing separation from the maternal, appeared after Bogan married Curt Alexander in 1916 and a year later traveled, four months pregnant, to the Panama Canal Zone, where Alexander was stationed with the Army. The poem figures a break from maternal attachment. To be betrothed is, perhaps, to betray the mother. As a speaker within the poem, a mother draws attention to the first painful cleaving of flesh in childbirth. Her suffering in childbirth becomes her "claim" upon her daughter, a possessive claim that she makes against a romantic ideal:

> My mother remembers the agony of her womb
> And long years that seemed to promise more than this.
> She says, "You do not love me,
> You do not want me,
> You will go away."
>
> In the country whereto I go
> I shall not see the face of my friend
> Nor her hair the color of sunburnt grasses;
> Together we shall not find
> The land on whose hills bends the new moon
> In air traversed of birds.
>
> What have I thought of love?
> I have said, "It is beauty and sorrow."
> I have thought that it would bring me lost delights, and splendor
> As a wind out of old time. . . .
>
> But there is only the evening here,
> And the sound of willows
> Now and again dipping their long oval leaves in the water.
>
> (*BE* 7)

Women in the poem are associated with traditional images of feminine sexuality (hair, womb, and moon), while the male displays aggression rather than intimacy through his actions toward the speaker, who remarks: "You have put your two hands upon me, and your mouth." When the speaker departs from a possessive Demeter-like mother and her woman friend, she encounters silence and emptiness. Yet as a young woman who has separated from a female interconnected realm, she emerges into an order without meaning. Without female presence, the poem suggests, a plenitude of experience appears at least temporarily impossible, and perception of nature is reduced to repetition. The poem's conclusion remains characteristically ambiguous as the imposed romantic figurations have been dispelled, and the woman is cast into a nearly silent landscape. Neither possessive mother nor romantic partner have captured the speaker's allegiance, and her isolation could hardly be more complete. The poem's syntax and diction, at points archaic, underscore the speaker's early sentimentalized idealization of experience. The language alters, however, at the close of the poem, turning spare and quiet, and Bogan seems most determinedly modernist in the final stanza as she focuses on an uninscribed landscape. Although we might note here the Pre-Raphaelite sensuousness in the long *o* sounds of the last lines, the lines nevertheless pull us not only to a conception of loss but to a drift into meaninglessness and modernist alienation.

What is finally left to the young woman but the crossed gift of memory? In a sense, the poem has been an exercise in memory, a review of a woman's past that encloses her own mother's recollections: "My mother remembers the agony of her womb." Indeed, the question of memory in this context becomes urgent. "For people like myself to look back is a task," Bogan observes in another context. "It is like re-entering a trap, or a labyrinth, from which one has only too lately, and too narrowly, escaped" (*JAR* 10). And for Bogan, mother and memory are somehow implicated with one another, as the poem "Memory" may suggest:

> Do not guard this as rich stuff without mark
> Closed in a cedarn dark,
> Nor lay it down with tragic masks and greaves,
> Licked by the tongues of leaves.
>
> Nor let it be as eggs under the wings
> Of helpless, startled things,
> Nor encompassed by song, nor any glory
> Perverse and transitory.

> Rather, like shards and straw upon coarse ground,
> Of little worth when found,—
> Rubble in gardens, it and stones alike,
> That any spade may strike.
>
> (*BE* 18)

In three movements the poem advances its implicit argument: memory should not be assigned high value, nor should it be preserved; instead, the persistent memory should be unvalued, for it obstructs growth—the growth of the individual and the growth of the poem. Yet, ambiguously, the poem betrays the speaker's wish that memory be readily available to consciousness. Any "spade," any act of writing, will "strike" memory. "Strike" here would seem not only to imply the act of striking out, of erasing, but its double meaning referring to discovery, for to strike is to find. Similarly, memory in the later poem "March Twilight" is marked by vacillations reminiscent of the mother, "the most desperate and kindest embrace," and recollection of the maternal is gained only fitfully: "A watcher in these new, late beams might well see another face / And look into Time's eye, as into a strange house, for what lies within" (*BE* 127).

Bogan distrusted memory not simply because she suffered from her own recollections and acknowledged that she was unable to recall essential events in her past, such as those surrounding her temporary childhood blindness, but because she believed that representation of memory falsified. Memory might recast and distort past events within both dream and waking life. Only through lyric poetry might she discover the necessary form to explore her past struggles in their fullest complexity. And in the poem— the text that resists the symbolic order's governance even while it occupies symbolic structures—she discovered an opportunity to evoke her fullest responses.

Another early poem, "The Changed Woman," embodies further rich complications. Although the poem's title might suggest contrition and even repression, for *the changed woman* is often enough a phrase used for a woman chastened by scandal, Bogan's central figure evolves from maintaining a willed suppression of her desires to expressing her own psychological reconstitution:

> The light flower leaves its little core
> Begun upon the waiting bough.
> Again she bears what she once bore
> And what she knew she re-learns now.

The cracked glass fuses at a touch,
The wound heals over, and is set
In the whole flesh, and is not much
Quite to remember or forget.

Rocket and tree, and dome and bubble
Again behind her freshened eyes
Are treacherous. She need not trouble.
Her lids will know them when she dies.

And while she lives, the unwise, heady
Dream, ever denied and driven,
Will one day find her bosom ready,—
That never thought to be forgiven.

(*BE* 22)

While "the cracked glass" and the healed wound "set / In the whole flesh"
are never entirely effaced from the body and the psyche, the woman must
gain strength through, paradoxically, her very vulnerability to the source of
obsessive materials. The poems' concluding lines suggest a new wounding
by aspiration. Simultaneously, "ever denied and driven," the dream is at
last harbored by the changed woman.

On one level, the poem is a transformed account of the poet's relationship with the maternal, experienced as inconstant and yet alluring in the
person of May Bogan, whose adulteries and abandonments of her family
not only marked Bogan's childhood but influenced her mature perceptions
and choice of subject matter. In this context, the seeming neutrality of the
images "Rocket and tree, and dome and bubble" take on significance as
threatening representations of sexual identity.[33] Passion is not simply hazardous, however, but here, even when beaten down and confined, reemerges
to become the woman's "unwise, heady / Dream." Although she cannot
expect forgiveness from her culture, or, perhaps, ready self-forgiveness,
the changed woman will resume her desires.

The poem points to the price of social ostracism that a woman who
follows her passions may face. In this context, Bogan's description in her
journal of her mother's reunion with her family after a mysterious extended
absence is revealing; May Bogan repeatedly fit the role of a changed woman:

Once, in Ballardvale, she was away for some weeks. No one knew where
she had gone. Then suddenly she came back, thinner and, as I remember, in
totally different (and shabby) clothes. She had a complete look of sorrow
and of contrition in her eyes. Her eyes were humble; they asked you to for-

give her. We forgave her instantly. She went about the house humbly and called us humbly by our names. She called (as she so rarely did) my father by his name. She swept and cleaned and changed the paper on the kitchen shelves. Then, after some days, she opened the piano and played and sang. And we (my brother and myself) sang with her. . . . (*JAR* 35)

"The Changed Woman" may have emerged in part from Bogan's attempt to understand obsessions that her mother only temporarily withstood before once more capitulating to desires that were denied fulfillment in more productive form by her society. The changed woman continues to change, repeating and relearning her lessons. She is, it would seem—for better or for worse—a woman of perpetual changes. While I have argued in chapter 1 that Bogan was a critic of the excesses of romantic love, particularly as its conventions subjugated women in a role of dependency, she was ultimately sympathetic to the desire for intensive feeling that was evinced in romantic love. In "The Changed Woman" desire is aligned with figures suggestive of sexuality, and yet the broad figurations in the poem suggest that the woman's desires may not be limited to sexual expression alone. However "unwise" and "heady" the woman's dream may be, eventually it is internalized by her and she assumes the role of a woman of redeemable life energy, despite the threat of social ostracism that she faces.

In her third collection, *The Sleeping Fury*, Bogan assumes the maternal voice in the face of the malice of the Yeatsian "Paudeens" who condemn illicit behavior. Her poetry takes on astringent tones as she explores afflictions of the sort that inevitably contributed to her mother's unhappiness. Bogan was herself bedeviled by her belief that her own reputation, like her mother's, was subject to vicious rumors. When first offered the chance to meet W. H. Auden (whose work she admired and whom she later befriended), she feared that he was interested in her only as a subject of scandal for her early and brief romantic connection to the "social activist-thief" John Coffey.[34] Her poems of malice, many of them written when Bogan was experiencing acute psychological distress, further reflect her identification with her mother, who needed to be defended against townspeople critical of her behavior. She wrote of her childhood reactions to the treatment her mother received:

I had early been stamped by the exigent demands of a childish loyalty. The beauty and arrogance close to me often met sneers and rebuffs from the less endowed beings about her. Early I saw them jib and sneer. Early, early, from the beginning, I abjured the ordinary world. (*JAR* 57)

The account reflects Bogan's attempt to make sense of her conflicted loyalties. Ultimately, she would identify with her mother's "beauty and arrogance," renouncing what she viewed as middle-class conventions.

At the time that she was writing *The Sleeping Fury* Bogan was increasingly contemplating the nature of loss—of both Raymond Holden and, in another sense, of her mother, for she had experienced at an early age the loss of a stable maternal image. As we have seen in chapter 2, Bogan's responses to psychological loss were complex and involved questions of repression and expression. In her notebooks she copied out many quotations from books on psychoanalysis, apparently as a means to achieve greater understanding of her own psyche. Her notes from Otto Fenichel's *Outline of Clinical Psychoanalysis* may be particularly helpful to us:

> A grief-stricken person who has lost an object must loosen the libidinal attachment that binds him to it. This tie is not a matter of a single situation; the libido is attached to thousands of individual memories; and on each of the[se] memories the dissolution of the tie must be carried through, *which takes time* [Bogan's emphasis]. This process Freud designated the "grief-work" *(Trauerarbeit)*. It is comparable to the "working through" *(Durcharbeiten)* that takes place in a therapeutic analysis, wherein a certain interpretation is brought to bear successively on all the individual manifestations of a given idea. The carrying out of the grief work is a difficult and unpleasant task, which many persons try to evade for a time by employing repression, so that the apparent lack of emotion may be due in part to an identification with the dead person.[35]

She does not copy Fenichel's next observations, but they too seem cogent. He goes on to state that mourners may assume certain qualities of "the lost object." Fenichel notes, "It can often be observed that the mourner in one or another respect comes to resemble the lost object: that for example, as Abraham reported, his hair may become gray like the hair of the person he mourns, that he may develop cardiac symptoms if the person died of heart disease, that he may assume his peculiarities of speech or gesture in one or another way, and the like."[36] Identification with the mother may have been highlighted through Bogan's own insistence on viewing herself, like her mother in youth and early middle age, as a woman of trespass.

Significantly, in "Exhortation" Bogan opposes a stubbornly malicious social world that would seem to be a refraction of the social world that condemned her mother's behavior:

> The dead, long trained to cruel sport
> And the crude gossip of the grave;

The dead, who pass in motley sort,
Whom sun nor sufferance can save.
Face them. They sneer. Do not be brave.

Know once for all: their snare is set
Even now; be sure their trap is laid;
And you will see your lifetime yet
Come to their terms, your plans unmade,—
And be belied, and be betrayed.

(*BE* 67)

As Bogan informed Sister M. Angela, "Exhortation" was composed "on the verge of a psychic and physical breakdown (which had roots in reality, and partook v. little of fantasy)."[37] She emphasized that her sense of betrayal evolved from actual experience rather than from delusion. The final line of "Exhortation" links the poem to the first site and practice of betrayal: the mother.

A tone of distrust similarly pervades a number of poems in the first section of *The Sleeping Fury*, suggesting Bogan's suspicions of her associates in a way that duplicates her mother's apparent wariness toward her own associates. Bogan evokes revulsion and briefly recreates an atmosphere of betrayal in "At a Party":

Spirit (and let the flesh speak out),
Be still. To make this moment mine
All matter falls into a rout;
Both art and usury combine.

And each bright symbol of their power
Speaks of my triumph, and your fall.
Step forth, then, malice, wisdom's guide,
And enmity, that may save us all.

(*BE* 70)

In another key, "Henceforth, From the Mind" reveals her disillusion at this stage, and her fear of renunciation—for if only the mind, unrooted in bodily pleasure, is the source of joy, speech itself turns hollow, and experience would be an echo removed from its central source. As each stanza concludes, Bogan would seem quietly to mourn a sealed fate. The final stanza hints at the losses entailed in any pursuit limited to the mind, for while Bogan tends to use fairly realistic images, even in her poems detailing dreams, here the images foreground fragmentation and diminishment:

> The shadow of increase,
> Will sound you flowers
> Born under troubled peace—
> Henceforth, henceforth
> Will echo sea and earth.
>
> (*BE* 64)

Flowers are not born, neither do they sound. And peace is hardly peace if it is troubled.

"Hypocrite Swift," a poem that Bogan wrote while recovering from a breakdown in 1931, castigates this sort of renunciation and sterility both in the social world and within the self: the Jonathan Swift of this poetry (like the maternal for Bogan) both suffers and creates suffering for others while he endures his own disenchantment. She explained to Edmund Wilson: "*The Journal to Stella* wrung my heart. The passion is so real, so imperfectly dissembled, and the wit is such a strange mixture of roughness and elegance."[38] The sixth stanza signals a new depth of feeling in its acceleration and condensation of images and conceptual unities.

> On walls at court, long gilded mirrors gaze.
> The parquet shines; outside the snow falls deep.
> Venus, the Muses stare above the maze.
> Now sleep.
>
> (*BE* 68–69)

In a reflective, quieted, and isolated sphere, archetypal presences intervene as witnesses: "Venus, the Muses stare above the maze." By connecting the goddess of love with the goddesses of the arts, Bogan puts forward an essential and elemental condensation: love and art conflate in her struggle with past phantoms.

> Dream the mixed, fearsome dream. The satiric word
> Dies in its horror. Wake, and live by stealth.
> The bitter quatrain forms, is here, is heard,
> Is wealth.
>
> What care I; what cares Saucy Presto? Stir
> The bed-clothes; hearten up the perishing fire.
> Hypocrite Swift sent Stella a green apron
> And dead desire.

Swift's appetites exclude greater intimacy. As many of her critics have noted, Bogan may have been responding to the lack of feeling that she experienced at this juncture in her life; her own "dead desire" threatened to stifle creativity and, she feared, love.

Through "stealth," Bogan's Swift would escape the responsibility of love and obscure his failure in wit. Words are the cloak and mask of this figure of denial, defending against an overbearing paranoiac anxiety. Bogan's own anxiety filters through the capillaries of the poem. And in gilded quatrains she dramatizes her sense of division. As "two different clocks, here and in Dublin, / Give out the hour" (*BE* 68) for Swift, Bogan similarly experiences a breach in time and place as her need to be "put back together again" intensifies. She believed that her "rapid recovery" from mental breakdown occurred once she realized—in the very process of composing "Hypocrite Swift"—that she was actually writing mature poetry again.[39]

Despite lacerating ironies, "Hypocrite Swift" is an expression of Bogan's identity as a poet, and she could be justly proud of the technical intricacy of the poem's variations on the Sapphic stanza with the added challenge of rhyme. Eventually she came to see the time she spent in recovery from breakdowns as part of a larger scheme; her illnesses initiated a necessary struggle. Two years after the publication of *The Sleeping Fury* she wrote to Zabel: "Madness and aberration are not only parts of the whole tremendous set-up, but also, I have come to believe, *important* parts. Life trying new ways out and around and through. The only bad kind of pain and aberration is the kind caused by power wanting to come through, and being pushed back. Then you get suffering, and if it isn't used to grow, it thumps one right back into the bassinet. . . . "[40] In the same year she speculated in a letter to Rolfe Humphries that "Perhaps madness, like cancer, is a way of life trying to transcend itself."[41]

One of her more ambitious poems in *The Sleeping Fury* tests romantic enthrallment and rejects self-betraying eroticism. In such a rejection she focuses on temptations that had erupted for both her mother and herself and transcends them. "Putting to Sea" is about "power wanting to come through" and the self-deluding obstacles to a deeper psychic immersion. Bogan wrote to Wheelock that the poem "will sum up the Holden suffering, endured so long, but now, at last, completely over."[42] Rather than romantic attachment, her speaker chooses the uncharted depths of the unconscious. She withdraws from bodily deception to allow formerly unconscious impulses to enter consciousness. Bogan's traveler must leave behind her past, the site of betrayal. While threatening to destroy her bearings, the ocean nevertheless may release her from stupefying and self-denying passion:

> "O, but you should rejoice! The course we steer
> Points to a beach bright to the rocks with love,
> Where, in hot calms, blades clatter on the ear;
>
> And spiny fruits up through the earth are fed
> With fire; the palm trees clatter; the wave leaps.
> Fleeing a shore where heart-loathed love lies dead
> We point lands where love fountains from its deeps.
>
> Through every season the coarse fruits are set
> In earth not fed by streams." Soft into time
> Once broke the flower: pear and violet,
> The cinquefoil. The tall elm tree and the lime
>
> Once held out fruitless boughs, and fluid green
> Once rained about us, pulse of earth indeed.
> There, out of metal, and to light obscene,
> The flamy blooms burn backwards to their seed.
>
> With so much hated still so close behind
> The sterile shores before us must be faced;
> Again, against the body and the mind,
> The hate that bruises, though the heart is braced.
>
> Bend to the chart, in the extinguished night
> Mariners! Make way slowly; stay from sleep;
> That we may have short respite from such light.
>
> And learn, with joy, the gulf, the vast, the deep.

(*BE* 84–85)

The traveler attempts to pass beyond the already known demands of the sensual body, not out of fear, as in "The Frightened Man," but as a necessary response to an unbalanced bodily economy; she had been moored in unstable and obsessive desires. The images in part are those of "The Tale" and seem to be derived from her experience as a disillusioned young wife in the Panama Canal Zone. She faces again the sources of her disillusionment, and the closing isolated line floats her desire—not for arrival on shore, but for an encounter with the sea of the unconscious as it may now be realized as healing, "vast," and "deep." Bogan concludes by presenting the poetic self as an explorer of the unconscious who will not be waylaid by the continued force of the past or by the siren calls of romance preying on natural appetites.

Early reviewers of *The Sleeping Fury* largely ignored poems dissecting malice in social relations and repudiating obsession. Kenneth Rexroth, despite his assertion that her earlier books are invested with "a penetrating and profoundly disturbing quality, a force of acid insinuation rather than impact," found *The Sleeping Fury* to be a quiescent book.[43] "Supposedly this is what is called mellowing, this is matured wisdom, and Miss Bogan's style has mellowed with it. . . . Doubtless this is in many ways a better book, but something very valuable is going from Miss Bogan's talent, and nothing new but 'wisdom' is coming to replace it."[44] Allen Tate believed the poetry was "purer" than that of Edna St. Vincent Millay's and Elinor Wylie's.[45] Ford Madox Ford considered the poems to be "authentic," that is, "intimately sympathetic and satisfactory."[46] Perhaps predictably, most often it was Bogan's command of form that arrested the attention of her critics rather than the complexity of her responses to circumstance.

The volume's two poems that deal directly with acts of creation and destruction note the necessity for rupture of form. Pitting symbolic order against maternal creativity and the claims of the mother, Bogan confronts the pretensions of poetic immortality as opposed to the fleshly urgency of the body in *The Sleeping Fury*. In "Homunculus" a figure is composed beyond the realm of a parent's flesh and, as a consequence, "lacks but life," the essential without which the speaker's boasts ring hollow. The homunculus engages neither maternal nor paternal body. Bogan assaults artificial unity, the unruptured sensibility "joined / More cleanly than a thorn," for ultimately "life" involved at least the intuition of the splitting of figurations, some initial account of a break from a maternal source:

> O see what I have made!
> A delicate precious ruse
> By which death is betrayed
> And all time given use.
>
> See this fine body, joined
> More cleanly that a thorn.
> What man, though lusty-loined,
> What woman from woman born,
>
> Shaped a slight thing, so strong,
> Or a wise thing, so young?

This mouth will yet know song
And words move on this tongue.

It lacks but life: some scent,
Some kernel of hot endeavor,
Some dust of dead content
Will make it live forever.

(BE 65)

The homunculus presents both a state of mind and a substance—and anything but desire. The homunculus is not a split being, nor has it caused a
rupture of the maternal body through childbirth. It remains divorced from
physicality and withdrawn from the feminine. The artificial form of the
homunculus ought to be shattered, Bogan suggests, just as artifice is shattered in its companion poem "Kept."

In the latter poem, Bogan depicts a break from artificial conceptions,
the breaching of securities. She intimates a break from the maternal, figured
in the toy and doll as the child's substitutes for the mother. Of course, in
much conventional psychology the toy is seen as a transitional object allowing the child to prepare for further separations from the mother. Through
her treatment of the doll and the toy, the child may duplicate aspects of her
relationship with her mother. In Bogan's poem toys undergo a necessary
fracturing:

What are these rags we twist
Our hearts upon, or clutch
Hard in the sweating fist?
They are not worth so much.
. . . .
Time for the pretty clay,
Time for the straw, the wood.
The playthings of the young
Get broken in the play,
Get broken, as they should.

(BE 87)

She suggests that we would cling to the familiar as we might, ironically,
cling to maternal presence. Rupture here proves inevitable as long as the
child plays, for playing is engaging with time, and time of course wears away
all things. Yet the poem's final lines, through repetition, intimate the plaintive loss of preoedipal unity, hinting at the very difficulty of this rupture.

Increasingly, Bogan perceived complex aesthetic form as a defense against the psychic disorder that plagued her and that appeared to her to be derived from childhood trauma. Achieved order, as we have seen, is present alongside disorder in her poems. In *The Sleeping Fury* she contemplates formal design in art more fully than in earlier collections. "Baroque Comment" renders formal control as coexisting with disorder, particularly with chaos caused by deception, weighted as lies were for Bogan with memories of her mother's deceptions. A catalog of humanly shaped materials in "Baroque Comment," first published in 1935 in the *New Yorker*, serves as a counterpoint to disorderly emotion and, pointedly, to "the lie, anger, lust, oppression, and death in many forms." From the metallic flower, sculpted stone, constellations rendered into language, and water shaped by fountains, the poet moves to extensions of the body in simple tools. She closes with the physical expressions of love:

> Crown and vesture; palm and laurel chosen as
>   noble and enduring;
> Speech proud in sound; death considered sacrifice;
> Mask, weapon, urn; the ordered strings;
> Fountains; foreheads under weather-bleached hair;
> The wreath, the oar, the tool,
> The prow;
> The turned eyes and the opened mouth of love.
>
>   (*BE* 76)

The ambiguity of Bogan's final images (Are the eyes turned for the lover's arrival or departure? Is the mouth open in spent passion or in unrequited longing?) reinforces our perception of the ambiguity and intricacy of artful form. Echoing such preoccupations, "Italian Morning" confronts mutability. In those ranges beyond sight ("In long perspective past our eye") one may intimate the extraordinary through ornament (*BE* 74). Similarly, in "Roman Fountain" the fountaineer's aim resembles the poet's goal to create form through which energy must rise. As the fountain rises, only a brief moment of peace occurs, for the water must "reach to its rest and fall" (*BE* 80). As such, the poem is not Bogan's static entity but a "fountain" of volatile processes.

    Through "intricate forms," Bogan declared that not only the heart must "cry out" but so too must the hand—the hand that writes the poem, as a journal entry records:

I thought again of the miracle of ornament: why did mankind throw up moldings and arabesques and intricate forms in wood and stone? Why was

not all this creative impulse expended upon poetry (the heart's cry), specula-
tion (the mind's search), or the pastime of story-telling alone? It was because the *hand* had to cry out as well as the heart. (*JAR* 97)

Bogan frequently connects aesthetic form to the image of the hand, by
extension linking form to the mother, for the hand is the synecdoche by
which the mother is most often identified in her writings. The mother herself, although an agent of familial disintegration, is linked to questions of
formal order. In a journal entry of 1959 that recalls the apple-bearing woman
of "The Crossed Apple," Bogan writes:

> My mother had true elegance of hand. She could cut an apple like no one
> else. Her large hands guided the knife; the peel fell in a long light curve
> down from the fruit. Then she cut a slice from the side. The apple lay on the
> saucer, beautifully fresh, white, dewed with faint juice. She gave it to me.
> She put the knife away. (*JAR* 28)

In this description Bogan images the mother's withheld violence as it may
be experienced simultaneously with formal control. Significantly, the hands
of her mother perform as aesthetic standards: "Their chief beauty lay in the
way they moved. They moved clumsily from the wrist, but intelligently
from the fingers. They were incapable of any cheap or vulgar gesture" (*JAR*
29). She describes the fracture in her mother's nature between destruction
and creation, defining her mother, while describing her hands, as both a
source of "terror" and "tenderness": "For the hands that peeled the apple
and measured out the encircling ribbon and lace could also deal out disorder and destruction. They could tear things to bits; put all their soft strength
into thrusts and blows; they would lift objects so that they became threats
of missiles" (*JAR* 29). A sense of sinister possibility emerges from frequent descriptions of her mother's hands, including a description from the
short story "Dove and Serpent": "She had large, beautiful hands, but when
she was tired or nervous she could not hold anything in them—everything
she touched tumbled to the floor" (*JAR* 5).

Recalling her mother's infidelities in a journal entry, Bogan isolates
"the ringed hand on the pillow" as a symbol of maternal betrayal and of her
own despair and loneliness as a child—notably as a child too young for the
consolations that reading and writing might afford:

> The door is open, and I see the ringed hand on the pillow; I weep by the hotel
> window as she goes down the street, with *another*; I stare at the dots which
> make up the newspaper photograph (which makes me realize that I then had

not yet learned to read). The chambermaid tells me to stop crying. How do we survive such things? But it is long over. And forgiven . . . (*JAR* 172)

When exploring her first childhood revelation of aesthetic form, Bogan imagines the independent work of her own hands. Her mother had been hospitalized for an operation, and the young Louise, with her father and brother, visited her. Apparently the hospital arrangements had been made by a doctor who was one of her mother's lovers. A bouquet of marigolds in the hospital room, contrasted in a journal entry to the pink hothouse roses given to May Bogan by the doctor, a "Yankee admirer," take on enriched meaning and allow this precocious child to grasp her own sense of meaningful shape and evocative design:

Suddenly I *recognized* something at once simple and full of the utmost richness of design and contrast that was mine. A whole world, in a moment, opened up: a world of design and simplicity; of a kind of rightness, a kind of taste and knowingness, that shot me forward, as it were, into an existence concerning which, up to that instant of recognition, I had had no knowledge or idea. *This* was the kind of flower, and the kind of arrangement and the sense of arrangement plus background, that, I at once realized, came out of impulses to which I could respond. I saw the hands arranging the flowers and leaves, the water poured into the vase, the vase lifted to the shelf on which it stood: they were my hands. (*JAR* 22)

Bogan imagines her hands arranging the bouquet, assuming a power that is entirely her own. Such a description allows us an opportunity to identify her early sense of formal properties and to contemplate the way in which she had already conceived of form as an arrangement that may be viscerally experienced. The passage not only suggests the child Bogan's rivalry with her mother's suitor (the source of the hothouse roses) and her transcendence of the painful situation provoked by her mother's hospitalization, but her own readiness to envision form as a means of self-enablement, of grasping an authority of vision and of acute visual and tactile command. In the collapse of what normally had been her mother's tremendous vitality, it may have been necessary for Bogan to discover for herself her own aesthetic sensitivity.

In 1954 Bogan wrote to May Sarton that she had "been forced to lose [her] life in order to find it." In her letter she related psychic survival to the urge to shape by using one's "spiritual *and* corporeal" hands:

At least twice in my present existence I have been forced to lose my life in order to find it. . . . This means losing people, for a time—and losing oneself—

getting to the point where one gives up *completely* and merely keeps breathing, hoping that the power and the will to live will come back. The power of *persons* is lessened, after such experiences. It is a sort of amputation, I am sure; but one can manage, if one's heart and brain haven't been cut off. And one's hands—spiritual *and* corporal. . . .[47]

It was important for Bogan to incorporate in her poetry those elements of her mother's legacy that were most positive: strong feeling and "true elegance," the latter evidenced, at least occasionally, by the work of her mother's hands. Yet increasingly she would reject former obsessions, as she explained to Sarton, for she believed that maturity—and even psychic survival—required a dissolution of obsessions.

In the title poem of *The Sleeping Fury* Bogan most fully creates a form for maternal energies and recognizes the maternal as a creative source. In particular, she ushers the maternal in "The Sleeping Fury" into the realm of art and archetype.

Her method of composition of "The Sleeping Fury" was, for her, an unusual one. She first drafted a prose version, writing of the sleeping Gorgon: "[I]t can be approached, gazed upon, even touched. It can draw pity from our hearts, and tenderness, as it lies in its solitude."[48] Pointedly, the fury is an object of pity, an emotion that Bogan reserved for both her mother and the child she remembered herself to be.

In the completed poem, she retains some of the prose version's expository elements, but the Fury more fully serves as Bogan's figure of revelation and awe. We might remember that in Greek mythology the Furies avenged crimes within the family or kinship group. They were said to create further disturbances within the mind; in addressing the Fury, then, Bogan alludes to familial wounds and conflates the maternal with mental distress. Destructive unless fully recognized and confronted, "Hands full of scourges, / wreathed with your flames and adders" (*BE* 78), the Fury may compel the release of repressed material through her enflamed and violent presence. Like the figure of "Cassandra" who would "bare the shambling tricks of lust and pride," the Fury is a revealer, bringing to awareness crimes within the family. The Fury bears characteristics evident in Bogan's descriptions of her mother: violence and vacillation merge with a childlike temperament. We may recall Bogan's description of her mother: "A terrible, unhappy, lost, spoiled, bad-tempered child," Bogan wrote, immediately appending: "A tender, contrite woman . . ." (*JAR* 35).

In "The Sleeping Fury" Bogan simultaneously addresses the acts of the betraying mother and the injured child, even as the Fury must uncover wrongdoing and apportion guilt. Significantly, the speaker pacifies the Fury with her own gaze. The dreadful muse, once confronted, reveals herself to be a familiar figure to Bogan: the child-self who had been manipulated into secrecy, "in the locked stillness of houses." Bogan frees herself from the position of traumatized child to meet and return the maternal gaze. Unlike the Medusa of her early poem, the sleeping Gorgon is not a monstrous other who destroys upon confrontation; instead, in this resolved crisis, confrontation appeases the Fury, herself a revised Medusa-like figure, her hair "in the semblance of serpents," but her gaze, before she sleeps, now assuming the dynamics of an activating, freeing force.

Rather than being harried by revelatory powers, the poet turns to confront the Fury's powers to impel and to witness change, and she channels them into refined shape. Indicating that this is a drama of sight, Bogan repeats the verb *look* in the final lines. And because the meeting is a mutual exchange of gazes, differentiation is made possible. Bogan does not reclaim the maternal so much as recognize the mother in clarified form and, in an exchange of identities, at last captures the "sliding eye" of the mother whom she perceived to be deceptive and whom she alluded to in the uncollected poem, "The Lie": "First met when I was young: / Within the sliding eye, / Upon the sidling tongue / I knew the lie."[49] The Fury, at last, is allowed peace from her own relentless need to scourge; yet she is not, as we should note, in any way domesticated or dismissed. Bogan revises the script of early paralysis and allows the mother to attain rest, the daughter to attain subjecthood. The Fury, then, reveals but cannot shape experience; after revelation she is pacified in a childlike sleep. The speaker, however, stands in a dominant maternal position as she watches the sleeping Fury:

> Beautiful now as a child whose hair, wet with rage and tears
> Clings to its face. And now I may look long upon you,
> Having once met your eyes. You lie in sleep and forget me.
> Alone and strong in my peace, I look upon you in yours.
>
> (*BE* 79)

It is the speaker/daughter/poet—awake—who not only confronts truth but surpasses the Fury to name and create form.

Bogan's completion of *The Sleeping Fury* nearly coincided with her mother's death. The juxtaposition of two letters Bogan wrote within four days to Zabel reflects the connection between the Fury and her mother. Bogan had received a picture of a relief sculpture of a sleeping Fury that she had viewed in the Museo Nazionale della Terme in Rome:

The [picture of the] Fury came intact, and it is so beautiful that I cried.—I would have written you before this, but my mother took sick the night before last, and today I managed to persuade her to go to the hospital, and it is pneumonia.

If you could have seen the fight she put up, right to the last. But now she is a poor dying woman. I wish I could stop remembering her in her pride and beauty—in her arrogance, that I had to fight so—and now I feel it would have been better if I hadn't fought at all. Because under it all was so much love, and I had to fight that too.

I'll write soon, after this is over—after I stop feeling that Lucifer should have won. *The damned, niggardly, carroty, begrudging world!*[50]

A day after May's death, Bogan wrote again to Zabel, quoting the final stanza of Yeats's "Quarrel in Old Age":

My mother died yesterday afternoon —In death she looks terribly scornful and proud, but I think she loved up to the end.

All I could do, last night, was read Yeats' later poems, on what old age is, and what it does.

> Somewhere beyond the curtain
> Of distorting days
> Lives that lonely thing
> That shone before these eyes
> Targeted, trod like Spring.

Say a prayer for her. Her name is Mary.[51]

Characteristically, Bogan hopes to resist the ravages of memory ("I wish I could stop remembering her in her pride and beauty"), even while she recalls her early insistence on psychological separation. The social world, a realm that she often thought of during this period as coercive and scandalized by both her mother and herself, is reduced in a string of invectives that indicates her need to identify with her mother's resistance in her youth and early middle age to conventional social expectations.

Significantly, an indication of the benign maternal emerges among the poems in *The Sleeping Fury*, and it betrays Bogan's at least unconscious desire for preoedipal unity. "Evening-Star" concludes the fourth section of *The Sleeping Fury*, a section devoted to familial poems, including as it does "The Sleeping Fury" and "To My Brother" as well as "M., Singing," a poem inspired by Bogan's daughter.[52] Perhaps the closest to an unambiguous portrayal of maternal love that Bogan had ever written, "Evening-Star" evokes a feminine presence that is "shining without burning," requiring no countering symbol, but "wanting and breeding sighs only."

Light from the planet Venus, soon to set,
Be with us.

Light, pure and round, without heat or shadow,
Held in the cirrus sky, at evening:
Accompany what we do.

Be with us;
Know our partial strength.
Serve us in your own way,
Brief planet, shining without burning.

Light, lacking words that might praise you;
Wanting and breeding sighs only.

(*BE* 83)

The poem advances through linked sounds: *Venus* is linked with *Be with us* in the first stanza and in the opening line of the third. *Venus* further echoes in *cirrus* in the second stanza and *serve us* in the third. The repeated invocation, "Be with us," reflects a desire for unity without strife or stasis. As Jaqueline Ridgeway observes, the poem is influenced by the "Ave Maria," "bringing to mind the role of Mary as intercessor for women in conjunction with the significance of the Roman Goddess for whom the planet Venus is named."[53] The poem is, I suggest, an invocation to another Mary, her mother, and to a maternal principle that is prelinguistic, beneficent, and resisting representation.

Another brief poem in the same section establishes Bogan's imaginative legacy to her daughter Maidie and her willingness, as a mother, to grant power rather than to seek the torturous loyalty that she believed May Bogan demanded. Although in her journals Bogan made her mother a victim of a "baffled artist's despair," in *The Sleeping Fury* she renders her own daughter as an artist with the ability to release archetypes:

Now, innocent, within the deep
Night of all things you turn the key,
Unloosing what we know in sleep.
In your fresh voice they cry aloud
Those beings without heart or name.

(*BE* 82)

In "M., Singing" she allows her daughter access to unconscious archetypes—an access that she desired for herself.

After *The Sleeping Fury* Bogan was not to abandon composing poems that allude to the maternal, yet none of her final collections bears such a sustained identification with maternal energies or documents her own conflicts with the maternal as fully as her third book. But late in her life she imagined an abandoned child longing for the preoedipal state. Nearly thirty years after the publication of *The Sleeping Fury*, Bogan turned to an enactment of the preoedipal in "Little Lobelia's Song." The focus of the poem, a "child-visitant," plagued Bogan during a depression in which her mornings were filled with bouts of unrelieved weeping. She wrote to Rufina McCarthy Helmer in 1966 that "work-exorcism," more than medication, seemed to be useful in ridding herself of what appeared to be (as a note in parentheses on a draft of the poem indicates) "an autonomous complex."[54]

> *It* vanished at 10:30 A.M. today, and hasn't been back. Work at the typewriter seems to bore it. For all it wants to do is *weep*. O heavens, am I seeing the end of the tunnel, *at last*?[55]

Bogan transformed her "child-visitant" through the poem and in doing so provides us with an enigmatic portrait. Little Lobelia cries for the ultimate indivisibility of the preoedipal state. As the abandoned and unspeakable child, Lobelia's voice would disrupt the insular mother:

> I was once a part
> Of your blood and bone.
> Now no longer—
> I'm alone, I'm alone.
>
> Each day, at dawn,
> I come out of your sleep;
> I can't get back.
> I weep, I weep.
>
> Not lost but abandoned,
> Left behind;
> This is my hand
> Upon your mind.

(*BE* 132–33)

In a restricted language field, this nursery-rhyme-like poem with its dominant monosyllabics voices not only childlike yearning but recasts the memory of rupture from maternal presence. Bogan has written of other abandoned females, but here the voice utters speech peculiar only to itself.

In this context, Lawrence Lipking's study *Abandoned Women* is suggestive:

> No reading lasts forever. Hence the powerless always retain the right to deny legitimacy to the most powerful reading. Outcasts of the social and linguistic community, abandoned women speak an abrasive language of their own. The loss within them forces out a voice not quite like any man's, and sometimes nearer to a cry than to intelligible speech.[56]

If we use Lipking's formulation, Lobelia's voice would seem "nearer to a cry than to intelligible speech." Bogan contacts the preoedipal child in the poem, and out of her own physical and psychological difficulties in late life (her third breakdown and battles with failing health and blocked imaginative writing) she attempts recognition of this newly awakened child of the psyche who first bore the maternal furies. Her desire to place such a voice within a poem suggests a deeply rooted obsession with the mother-child relationship and her own capacity, no matter how anguishing, to contact unconscious energies.

Increasingly in her last decades Bogan focused on forgiveness: "'And all things are forgiven, and it would be strange not to forgive'—this Chekhov knew. Forgiveness and the eagerness *to protect*: these kept me from putting down the crudest shocks received from seven on. With my mother, my earliest instinct was to protect—to take care of, to endure" (*JAR* 172). The need to endure, a necessity that she repeatedly ascribed to the serious poet, informs Bogan's poems. For good or ill, she would not allow herself to justify her losses or failures by blaming her mother. Yet, as late as 1960, she was still contemplating the issue of "the bad mother":

> We must not bring back and describe "the bad mother"—"the Dragon mother"—in order to justify ourselves. Only to understand. —To hold the portrait of this evil figure unresolved, into age, is madness. It should be resolved in late youth. (The last Chinese box . . .) The artist must resolve it into art . . . the man of action into action . . . the philosopher into ideas. After a certain age one should glimpse it most often as a dream—or v. infrequently in *consciously* evoked meaning. . . . (*JAR* 167)

In her own case, "the bad mother" was most fully resolved into art. "[W]hen one lets go, and *recognizes* the stream on which we move as the same stream which moves us within—that it is time and the earth floating our blood and flesh, floating its own child—and stops fighting against the kinship, the light flows; peace arrives."[57] In a speech at Bennington College in

1962 Bogan argued that "Women still have within them the memory of the distaff and the loom—and, we must remember, the memory of the dark, cruel, wanton goddesses. But because woman rarely has gone over, in the past, to a general and sustained low complicity or compliance in relation to her companion, man, we can hope for her future" (*JAR* 158). The mother as a "dark, cruel, wanton" goddess proved a vital figure for Bogan, suggesting the intense vitality and haunting presence of her mother—and her mother's apparent capacity for cruelty. Despite whatever childhood traumas she endured, however, Bogan could recognize the power of the maternal by refusing to attach herself through "low complicity or compliance" to a masculine order.

4

Imagining Release:
The Later Poems

Three years before the publication of *The Sleeping Fury* Louise Bogan had already complained to Morton D. Zabel that she might renounce poetry altogether:

> With Eliot, I pronounce poetry a mug's game (I called it a gull's game for years). I can no longer put on the "lofty dissolute air" necessary for poetry's production; I cannot and I will not suffer for it any longer. With detachment and sanity I shall, in the future, observe; if to fall to the ground with my material makes me a madwoman, I abjure the trade. Having definitely given up alcohol and romantic dreams, having excised my own neurosis with my own hand, having felt the knife of the perfectionist attitude in art and life at my throat. . . ."[1]

After her third book of poetry appeared she would not again publish a complete single volume composed largely of new poems. *Poems and New Poems* was published in 1941, gathering seventy-two poems from previous collections with sixteen new poems, two of which were translations. A poetic silence followed for about seven years. *Collected Poems, 1923–1953* (1954) contained only three new poems. Her last collection, *The Blue Estuaries: Poems, 1923–1968* (1968), added only ten new poems to the body of her earlier work. Several of the new poems were retrieved from drafts of poems that had been abandoned, some for as long as two decades. Yet, despite her small late output, her new poetry loosened earlier rhythmic and psychological strictures. Indeed, for Bogan to write poems after her three single collections were published required a change in perspective. It meant, in effect, a dispelling of previous habits and preoccupations for a poet who had made obsessive materials the core of her art and the source of the lyric. Explicitly she would now connect poetic composition with physical and psychological release. Release, the act of relinquishing obsessive materials and

117

dissolving corporeal constraints, would become the theme of much of her later poetry.

Bogan's almost chronic inability to write poems during the final decades of her life often has been discussed. Ruth Limmer points out, "[O]ne must weigh against her undeniable independence the fact that in her last two decades she wrote almost no poetry whatever. . . . The talent remained, but she had so hemmed it in that translation and criticism finally became almost her only creative outlet."[2] A similar diagnosis of self-constriction dominates other discussions of Bogan's failure to write more poetry. Tillie Olsen has referred to Bogan as "one of our most grievous 'hidden silences.' (Woman, economic, perfectionist causes—all inextricably intertwined.)"[3] Her silences have been explained as a consequence of her demanding professional life, a suspect perfectionism, and, as Gloria Bowles argues, "a strict idea of what a woman poet could and could not permit herself."[4]

Bogan as an artist was greatly self-aware, and her methods of composition grew out of convictions about the compressed lyric as it might be produced by women or men. Her decline in poetic production by the time she reached her early forties was deeply troubling to her, and she herself suggested that its roots were many. Surely, as many readers have noted, her life as a woman of letters had been demanding. And her relatively poor finances and her psychological health (delicate since she was in her twenties) undoubtedly added to her difficulties as a poet. The blow of her mother's death, following so closely upon her completion of *The Sleeping Fury*, may also have contributed to her silences.[5]

As early as 1936 Bogan was casting about for exemplars of lyric poets who prospered as they aged, for too often both genders suffered decline even in early middle age. She wrote to Wheelock of her relief upon finding Stéphane Mallarmé's *Poésies*, consisting of roughly fifty poems. "If that was his lifetime work, I haven't done so badly, at 38. And I cannot, as you know, write imitation poetry."[6] For Bogan it was perhaps her unwillingness to repeat herself and to feign an encounter with unconscious impulses that made writing poetry particularly difficult as she aged. And the demands that writing poetry made on her psychological balance were, perhaps, extreme. The sort of poetry that she wanted to compose could not, she believed, be counterfeited. By its very nature such poetry required the discipline of a certain reticence. In her early twenties she had written of the "true artist's" need to "vow" to pursue high aspirations, writing only when compelled to expression. She argued in "The Springs of Poetry" that the poet should be "completely blessed by that reticence celebrated by the old prophetic voice: 'I kept silent, even from good words . . . The fire kindled, and at the last, I spoke with my tongue.' Under the power of such reti-

cence, in which passion is made to achieve its own form, definite and singular, those poems were written that keep an obscure name still alive, or
live when the name of their author is forgotten."[7] Her words were written
in 1923 for a special issue of the *New Republic* on poetry. In that same issue
her first book was reviewed by A. Donald Douglas, who pointed to her
intense reticence as a form of accomplishment and praised her as an artist
who did not "carve the dragons' teeth into quaint toys and sell them in the
market."[8] Notably for Bogan, reticence did not mean suppression of emotion or a wariness about revealing the demands that fully experiencing each
stage of human growth required. "I don't think it a virtue to always be on
your guard, in any art," she wrote. "Reticence, yes, but not guardedness;
there's a difference."[9] Indeed, Bogan's tone of high aspiration as it is linked
to reticence was fulfilled in her work and in some ways distinguished it.
While there are relatively few final poems, the poems that we do have are
set in the body of the work as remarkable culminating moments. The later
poems move outward toward nature, diffusing a self in nature, and creating
a transparency of effect. At points the poems express a nearly objective
detachment about human aging that seemed to Bogan only possible to fully
imagine and express in the person of middle or old age. And whatever her
difficulties, the act of writing poetry continued to be of supreme interest to
her. In 1954 Bogan wrote to May Sarton, "[T]he work is really, for us, the
important thing. The channels must be kept open so that it may live and
grow."[10] And in 1962 she noted to Sarton with some pride, "I have been
writing since 1912, the year of your birth!"[11] Never given to abundant production, she managed to compose final lyrics that stand as testimony of her
stature as a lyric poet of genius in her later life.

In her earlier explorations of romantic betrayal and through her chart-
ing of the effects of repression, Bogan created poetry of powerful resonance. In her final decades she continued to develop, however painfully
and slowly, as a poet of major importance. From the beginning of her career she had been concerned with dramatizing or enacting states of obsession and release. The final poems modulate toward the latter, most often
rendering into new form her sense of the mysteries attendant upon her development as a woman. Bogan's final work defeats her own self-criticism,
at least momentarily, by transforming phantoms of repetition into images
and acts of release. Such a process moves beyond the reenactments of past
trauma.

"All has been translated into treasure," Bogan wrote in "After the Persian," and indeed the later poems would seem to operate on a principle
analogous to translation, "carrying across" meaning from the realm of the
unconscious to consciousness, transforming symbols, and bringing to light

the experience of loss and a process of gaining knowledge that she believed necessary for spiritual survival. These are highly patterned poems; some are executed in free verse but are formalistic in their concern for alliteration, assonance, and the telling pause.

Silence in the late poems becomes not only a background to Bogan's achievement but an element of that achievement. In this context, Mary K. DeShazer's examination of silence in Bogan's poetry is particularly meaningful. DeShazer observes that "Bogan's silent voice is a poetic device by which she attains power and yet acknowledges her conflict" and that "silence and solitude . . . are the central images of her most revealing poems about the muse."[12] Silence proves a powerful oppositional and subversive strategy, and a crucial component of "self-apotheosis."[13] In "Poem in Prose," for instance, a lover is described in terms of his physical beauty. He is "absorbed" into the speaker's "strength," her "mettle": "in me you are matched, and . . . it is silence which comes from us" (BE 72). The lover will not become the facile subject of a poem but instead must be the speaker's "secret." The poem's speaker thus reveals her feelings for him indirectly, through suggestiveness, and the speaker sees her silence as "virtue," as a "match" for her lover's presence. The poem opposes the demarcations of identity assigned through language. But of course Bogan must use words to make her claim and to assert the power of identification (and surely the power of the mind's "desperate esteem," which will eventually insist on her independence from this lover). The result is a form of identification in which both lovers defy the symbolic order much in the way that the poems of the maternal suggest an aspect of preoedipal union. In her last poems, in particular, Bogan makes silence a part of her aesthetic method as obsessive materials are repositioned and their genesis questioned. In later poems, as we shall see, silence is an attendant force, signifying in part a refusal of narrow reason. In early poetry she favored moments of silence within agonistic context; in later poetry her references to silence allude more fully to an acceptance of mortality.

Among the new poems in *Poems and New Poems*, Bogan progresses from the chiding spirit of "Several Voices Out of a Cloud," in which the laurel is denied to "Parochial punks, trimmers, nice people, joiners true blue," to allude in other poems to her periods of silence and, at last, of speech (BE 93). "Musician," for instance, through its envelope stanzas and repetition of light *i* sounds, dramatizes a moment of nearly erotic emancipation and accomplishment after a lengthy lull in creativity:

> Where have these hands been,
> By what delayed,
> That so long stayed
> Apart from the thin
>
> Strings which they now grace
> With their lonely skill?
> Music and their cool will
> At last interlace.
>
> (*BE* 106)

Other new poems suggest mysteries beyond rationality. The artist-naturalist's glass flowers in "Animal, Vegetable and Mineral" (to be discussed later in greater detail) thwart comprehension, as does the division between appearance and behavior that "Question in a Field" makes explicit:

> Pasture, stone wall, and steeple,
> What most perturbs the mind:
> The heart-rending homely people,
> Or the horrible beautiful kind?
>
> (*BE* 97)

Thoreau's statement that "there are few or no bluish animals" prompts Bogan to ponder the observation further in the two triplets of "Variation on a Sentence":

> (Buff kine in herd, gray whales in pod,
> Brown woodchucks, colored like the sod,
> All creatures from the hand of God.)
>
> And many of a hellish hue;
> But, for some reason hard to view,
> Earth's bluish animals are few.
>
> (*BE* 99)

The anomaly interests her; like the poet who is granted the laurel in "Several Voices," the blue animal remains curiously isolated. In the more ambitious poems, "The Dream" and "Evening in the Sanitarium," she transforms experience to suggest opposed forces and outcomes. The psychic demon may be appeased and encountered in "The Dream," and yet only false placation awaits women who suffer in "Evening in the Sanitarium."

Tellingly, *Poems and New Poems* closes with "The Daemon," presenting composition as a compulsion that must be obeyed:

> Must I speak to the lot
> Who little bore?
> It said *Why not?*
> It said *Once more.*

(*BE* 114)

"The Daemon," like "The Musician," asserts the essential force of the creative principle in spite of recurrent silences in Bogan's creative life. She wrote to Sarton: "'The Daemon' . . . was written *(given!)* one afternoon almost between one curb of a street and another. *Why not?* is always a great help. God presses us so hard, often, that we rebel—and we should. Auden once told me that we should *talk back* to God; that this is a kind of prayer."[14] By acknowledging daemonic energies, she maintains a precarious balance between the leaden petrifications of Medusa and the brandishing scourges of the Fury. And she reveals the insistence of the repressed once released, for the energies of the unconscious translated into the lyric do not demand ultimate and absolute mastery, she suggests, so much as the poet's willingness to recognize their potency and to respond imaginatively.

In the context of her later poems, Bogan's response to surrealism may be especially illuminating. In 1939 she wrote an essay on Paul Eluard for the *Partisan Review* in which she took the opportunity to attack much of surrealist practice. Although her readers might have been surprised to find Bogan sympathetic to dada, she argued that by departing from dada, particularly in abandoning its "far more vigorous assault against logic and the weight of bourgeois ideals," surrealism assumed an enervating and restrictive function that led to self-protectiveness for the artist. "It [dada] was able to laugh at its own jokes, be cynical with its own cynicism and cruel to its own sadism, and its dogmatic and persecutory symptoms were mild, if they existed at all."[15] Surrealism, on the other hand, provided sterile cerebral effects, as she would argue in another context decades later: "[T]he subconscious, when dredged up without skill or imagination, can be every bit as tiresome as the conscious."[16] While in a 1939 review of Muriel Rukeyser's poetry she was willing to cite at least the "brilliant snapshot technique of Surrealism"[17] (small praise given the superficiality she must have afforded to thinking of any poem as a snapshot), she found surrealism to be a source of empty artificiality. She was surely an avowed admirer of the most disciplined and arduous writers, among them the symbolist

Mallarmé, and as such she could hardly summon enthusiasm for copious automatic writing. She found surrealist practice especially antithetical to emotion, and she held that automatism offered little chance for creative tension, that is, for the interplay between elemental impulse and conscious craft that she believed must follow upon the upwelling of unconscious energies. The craft that she had honed laboriously as a teenager and later as an autodidact of literary traditions in English, French, and German would seem of little use in surrealist practice. Surrealism denied poetic workmanship, the arsenal of effects and "tools of her trade." In her journal she was entirely frank: "Surrealism bores me. My gift depended on the flash—on the *aperçu*. The fake reason, the surface detail, language only—these give no joy" (*JAR* 173–74).

Her opposition to surrealism may seem odd in the light of her own stated concern with the unconscious and her inclination to write of dream states. Indeed, I have been arguing that some of her poems perform as partial representations of a topographical model of the unconscious. Yet she felt—however much the reputed aims of dealing with unconscious energies were lauded in surrealism—that André Breton's manifestos opposed the core of her art, perhaps all the more so because of surrealism's superficial resemblance to her aims. Particularly in her essay on Eluard, a poet whom she had translated out of admiration, she took the opportunity to dismiss surrealism, for she believed Eluard's insistence on following the dictates of surrealism deformed his natural talents. Furthermore, she believed surrealists' emphasis on psychic freedom, evidenced in automatic writing, called up compensatory restrictions in the artist. Breton's manifestos led to the excommunication of followers and further restrictions upon discovery. Indeed, surrealism, she argued, came in under false pretenses: "It was announced by a call to order, disguised as a manifesto for more freedom."[18] With uncharacteristic hyperbole she called surrealism "a dogma equally unyielding, and in many ways parallelling Communist dogma."[19] If surrealists were to unite symbolist evocation with Freudian insight the movement would have proved liberating. But while surrealism derived its name from Apollinaire, it "deleted almost entirely" Apollinaire's "wit and pathos" and proved "from the beginning out for the dead-end effects of madness and mystification."

Somewhat surprisingly, Bogan cast her essay on Eluard in terms of psychological illness. Dada, which she is at some pains to defend, produces the more acceptable "hysteria of an intelligent living entity suffering from shock," whereas surrealism manifests "paranoia" and "psychosis."[20] Such psychological terms—given Bogan's two emotional breakdowns in the 1930s and subsequent hospitalizations—underscore the antipathy with which she regarded surrealism, as if the "invective" that she found in Breton's manifestos was similar to the invective that she sought to expunge from her own character.

The conclusion of the first part of her essay on Eluard proves one of the most damning critiques of surrealism by an important modern poet. It is particularly of interest in that it comes from a poet who took the unconscious as a route to her own maturation as a poet:

> The truth is, that in Surrealism, the dream is treated in the most primitive way: it is recounted or imitated; Surrealist poets have gone into the subconscious as one would take a short trip into the country, and have brought back some objects of grisly or erotic-sadistic connotation, or a handful of unrelated images, in order to prove their journey. It has not occurred to them that the journey has been taken many times, that human imagination has, before this, hung a golden bough before the entrance to hell, and has described the profound changes the true journey brings about. It is a journey not to be undertaken lightly, or described without tension of any kind.[21]

The passage betrays Bogan's sense that the surrealists trespassed as tourists too readily—and seemingly with too few consequences—upon territory in which she believed herself to have been transformed. While she was at times painfully aware of her own imaginative silences, she portrays the surrealists as choosing superficial fluency rather than profound struggle.

Bogan closed the first section of her essay with a mythological image of the golden bough that Aeneas grasped before his entry into the underworld—an image that served her as a reprimand to surrealist presumption. In Bogan's own use of mythological figures (Medusa, Cassandra, Leda, Danaë, Daphne) she not only draws upon traditional mythology but reconfigures its heroines for modern consciousness. Indeed, her descriptions of mythology might be linked to her aims for her own poetry and its resistance to contamination by surrealist practices. Her focus on myth in another essay may make clear her sense that surrealists arrogantly denied earlier discoveries about the unconscious:

> It [myth] is saturated with meaning; no matter how deeply we explore it, an irreducible residue of unconscious allusiveness remains inexplicable in any terms but the original legendary ones.[22]

Her own poems mimic the symbolic condensations of myth, dramatizing change at the deepest levels of the psyche. Indeed, she saw the latter effect—the transformation of the individual—as the very heart of myth: "Before the hero [in mythology] takes on full responsibility, full guilt, he must at least once face up to insoluble mystery, be completely humiliated, or be changed into a compelling 'opposite.'"[23] While her friend Theodore Roethke productively would present images suggestive of surrealist influence, exciting many of his readers, Bogan's rejection of all surrealist influence and her adherence to high formal art and to a specific vocabulary of images would seem to mark her as "out-of-fashion" in coming decades. Nor would she ally herself later with the confessional poets as they emerged at the end of the 1950s. "We're not here to expose each other," she wrote in her journal, "like journalists writing gossip, or children blaming others for their own bad behavior. And open confession, for certain temperaments (certainly for my own), is not good for the soul, in any direct way. To confess is to ask for pardon; and the whole confusing process brings out too much self-pity and too many small emotions in general" (*JAR* 10). She preferred the route of Emily Dickinson and certain mystics: "They document life's fearful limitations from which they suffer, but they do not mix self-pity with the account of their suffering which they describe, like their joy, in close detail."[24] For her, "close detail" amounted to the depiction of the psychological "grain" of events transformed into symbols. Her resistance to direct biographical statements within her work would seem repressive to later feminist critics who were especially interested in the way women poets more directly depicted their domestic and political situations. Yet Bogan's poems portray a release from psychological constraints that are not figured simply in individual or cultural terms but absorb both, and that even now can be heard, in another key, in contemporary poets such as Louise Glück and Gjertrud Schnackenberg, themselves poets of high accomplishment. In yet another key, we may hear echoes of her strategies in the poetry of Jean Valentine, which, while not cast in a traditional formal mode, makes similar use of spare context and points of silence.

Bogan's next book after *The Sleeping Fury*, *Poems and New Poems*, registers her preoccupation with the shapes of experience, culminating in dread and wonder. Art appears as a mystery of form—form that requires the conscious discipline and dedication of the craftsperson, while its substance must derive from sources antithetical to conscious reasoning. Notable in this context is "Animal, Vegetable and Mineral" (*BE* 94–96), her fantasia on cross-pollination as presented in the famous display of glass flowers in the Ware Collection of Harvard's Botanical Museum. The poem is a meditation on form that may remind us of Bogan's earlier focus on resistant psychological and artistic material and yet points ahead to her later poems in which speakers triumph over obsession. Technically the poem is highly complex: thirteen five-line stanzas with an elaborate rhyme scheme and a concluding line afloat in white space. In a sense, the poem is about enclosure and release as represented by the elaborate "dance" of cross-pollination. The poem includes ten parentheses, as if to mirror the enclosing actions referred to in the poem's descriptions of insects and plants and to suggest visually the powerful enclosing movements of formal poetry.

First published in the *Nation* in December 1940, the poem portrays reproduction in which the feminine ruthlessly fulfills its purpose. Working from a pamphlet about the work of the naturalist-artists Leopold and Rudolph Blaschka, Bogan transforms her source: what had been botanical prose for the general public becomes compact and evocative. She charts the regularity and precision of cross-pollination, effects that her poem both emulates and celebrates:

> Interdependence of the seed and hive!
> Astounding extraverted bee and flower!
> Mixture of styles! Intensity of drive!
> Both Gothic and Baroque blooms flaunt their power.
> The Classic *Empire* bees within them strive.
>
> (*BE* 94)

The substance of art is ultimately an opulent crossing of forms and energies: "Expectancy is constant; means are shifting" (95). The reader witnesses an economic (and expedient) arrangement, in fact, a spectacle of tension and release:

> What is the chain, then ask, and what the links?
> Are these acts sad or droll? From what derived?
> Within the floret's disk the insect drinks.
> Next summer there's more honey to be hived.
>
> (*BE* 96)

Within this ordered excess in which "both Gothic and Baroque blooms flaunt their power," a dance of violence and control takes place. The bee is pressed into the flower's service: "The bee's back, feet, head, belly have been drawn / Into the flower's plan for history." Through such "priming," release occurs: "The stigma profits, and the plant's at ease." The extraction of pollen may emancipate and overwhelm rationality. ("Here the mind's exceeded; / Wild intimations through the fibers shoot.") Cross-pollination prods thought (*think* or some version of the verb appears seven times) and provides an occasion, paradoxically, beyond thought, as art challenges comprehension: "What Artist laughs? What clever Daemon thinks?" (96).

Bogan further distinguishes between the desire to compose resonant forms of meaning and the contrary desire to adopt confining, socially acceptable "forms" of behavior in "Evening in the Sanitarium," another of the new poems in *Poems and New Poems*. The poem was first published as an imitation of Auden; surely it is more "peopled" than Bogan's other poems, and it unfolds scenically in a way that is unusual in her work. It is also more clearly a poem of direct social criticism than Bogan tended to write. But like her short stories "Hydrotherapy" (1931) and "Coming Out" (1933), both published in the *New Yorker*, the poem grew from her own experiences of hospitalization. Initially, the poem may appear to have little in common with those in which Bogan contemplates provocative natural or artificial form. Closer examination shows that it quietly introduces the subject of form, in this case constraint and disguise in form: "The free evening fades, outside the windows fastened with decorative iron grilles" (*BE* 111). In a subdued and regulated atmosphere, the patients appear (as does the speaker of the early poem "Medusa") to be petrified through superficial form. Their formal activities allow them to evade powerful feeling. "The complicated knitting," "the games of anagrams and bridge; / The deadly game of chess; the book held up like a mask": each pacifies (*BE* 111). The troublesome aspects of the women's lives are to be denied rather than confronted: "childhoods will be put away, the obscene nightmare abated" (*BE* 112). Formal activities neutralize these women's Furies, produce an inhibiting order, and prompt self-dread.

What is the alternative to madness for women who inspire dread in the conventional culture and who live in dread of their own emotions? The conventional alternative proves constricting: a deadly circuit of domestic routine. The wife must "return, return / To meet forever Jim home on the 5:35." In one of her more ironic observations on the failure of her culture to accommodate women's creativity, Bogan shows growth as limited to domestic form: "The fruit salad will bloom on the plate like a bouquet / And the garden produce the blue-ribbon aquilegia" (*BE* 111).

The poem's final stanza presents an opposition between psychological pacification, in the image of sanitarium baths, and psychological struggle in the image of the women's urge to determine, however gropingly, the approximate meaning of pressing form:

> At the ends of the corridors the baths are running.
> Mrs. C. again feels the shadow of the obsessive idea.
> Miss R. looks at the mantel-piece, which must mean
> something.

> (*BE* 112)

In the closing line we see a woman assuming a stance that may appear familiar to us by now; she gazes before her in an attempt to discern meaning. As in the early "A Tale" or the later "Masked Woman's Song," the identity of the gazer proves abraded and partial, and the task of actively shaping meaning is a dreadful confrontation with recalcitrant form. Miss R., it would seem, duplicates the poet's gaze, the gaze of the woman who determines that the shape before her "must mean something."

In "Zone," first published in *Poems and New Poems*, Bogan recasts and expands upon an earlier preoccupation, for the poem not only contains two of her signatures (a tropical landscape and the metaphor of cyclicity) but ends with notes on endurance—endurance of the past and endurance of the demands of her art:

> Like a ship, we have struck expected latitudes
> Of the universe, in March.
> Through one short segment's arch
> Of the zodiac's round
> We pass,
> Thinking: Now we hear
> What we heard last year,
> And bear the wind's rude touch
> And its ugly sound
> Equally with so much
> We have learned how to bear.

(*BE* 109)

"Zone" was one of Bogan's favorite poems, perhaps because it addresses a quality she prided herself upon: an acquired ability to withstand destructive forces. The poem's rhymes are loosely placed, and its short lines carry forward her quiet confirmation of a necessary schooling in endurance. In *Poet's Choice* she explains that the poem, composed in the late 1930s, arrived during "a transitional period both of [her] outward circumstances and [her] central beliefs."[25] Images within the poem reflect "those relentless universal laws, under which we live—which we must not only accept, but in some manner, forgive—as well as the fact of the human courage and faith necessary to that acceptance."[26]

For Bogan, art is finally what is earned in the face of such "relentless universal laws." "To an Artist, To Take Heart" further suggests endurance as the mark of the great artist. "Slipping in blood, by his own hand, through pride, / Hamlet, Othello, Coriolanus fall. / Upon his bed, however, Shakespeare died, / Having endured them all" (*BE* 104). As Bogan had reiterated early in her career, the act of composition involved experiencing violent feeling. "Sub Contra," one of her first published pieces, makes such violence clear. Upon the "thick chord of wonder" the poet must "beat . . . till it break" (*BE* 5). "Roman Fountain" echoes the same visceral and dynamic conception of her processes: "O, as with arm and hammer, / Still it is good to strive / To beat out the image whole, . . ." (*BE* 80). In "Sonnet" Bogan further asserts the act of composition as a contest. Her early poetry evokes confrontations in which "the desperate mind" would "be thrown / Straight to its freedom in the thunderous cloud" (*BE* 26). In another vein, in "Single Sonnet" she directly addresses poetic tradition, announcing her intention to master enduring form: "Bend to my will, for I must give you love" (*BE* 66). Her later poems most often acknowledge the aftermath of her decisions to engage in struggles with the recalcitrant materials of art. The violence implicit in the act of composing the poem is remembered, but another strategy supplements and sometimes supplants it. Now her speakers seldom protest their circumstances, for they have imagined a vivid new environment for themselves, and when they look backward to the past they rename and requestion their previous experience or possess it newly. They recognize the daemonic, as we saw earlier in "The Sleeping Fury," but they pursue forms of understanding that demand that they release some aspect of previous behaviors, figured in the giving of a part of the self or the diffusing of the self outward upon a natural landscape. And yet, while taking on the authority of wisdom they do not assert ultimate mastery of experience.

Bogan was adamant even in early middle age about confronting the sources of repression, as "The Dream," published in the *Nation* in February 1938, makes clear. Elsewhere describing what she called the "stages" in life, she noted "understanding" as an ultimate goal: "First, that it should be romantic, exciting; then, that it should be bearable; and at last, that it should be understandable! These are the stages which we go through, in forming our desires concerning life" (*JAR* 109–10). In "The Dream" she invests a monstrous form, a "terrible horse," with repressed fear and anger in her own attempt at self-understanding and, ultimately, self-control:

> O God, in the dream the terrible horse began
> To paw at the air, and make for me with his blows.
> Fear kept for thirty-five years poured through his mane,
> And retribution equally old, or nearly, breathed through his nose.
>
> Coward complete, I lay and wept on the ground
> When some strong creature appeared, and leapt for the rein.

> Another woman, as I lay half in a swound,
> Leapt in the air, and clutched at the leather and chain.
>
> Give him, she said, something of yours as a charm.
> Throw him, she said, some poor thing you alone claim.
> No, no, I cried, he hates me; he's out for harm,
> And whether I yield or not, it is all the same.

The shadow-self as powerful beast is only tamed through an act of strange generosity, for the woman must give the horse something belonging to her, releasing the glove as metonymy for the writing hand.

> But, like a lion in a legend, when I flung the glove
> Pulled from my sweating, my cold right hand,
> The terrible beast, that no one may understand,
> Came to my side, and put down his head in love.
>
> (*BE* 103)

The force of the unconscious is harnessed when the woman flings the glove from her right hand, that is, through releasing her hand to write the poem. In 1954 Bogan wrote to Sarton that "The Dream" was "a poem of victory and of release. The terrible power, which may v. well be the psychic demon, is tamed and placated, but NOT destroyed; the halter and the bit were already there, and something was done about *control* and *understanding*."[27] Finally, the horse is likened to "a lion in a legend," a figure made of language and a symbol familiar in art. Writing to Sister M. Angela, Bogan explained that she composed "The Dream" in her late thirties "after a complete change in my way of living, and in my general point of view about life (and the universe at large!). It is the actual transcript of 'a nightmare,' but there is reconciliation involved with the fright and horror. It is through the possibility of such reconciliation that we, I believe, manage to live."[28]

In both "The Dream" and "The Sleeping Fury" Bogan projects the power of confronting the sources of desires and fears. But only in "The Dream" does she mark the demonic force with something explicitly her own. The glove is pointedly not a sacrifice but a gift; "give him something of your own," insists an attending presence—significantly enough, a female double. With the glove's release, not only recognition occurs but a charmed gift is proffered, delivering the speaker from her stance of fearful withdrawal and arid isolation. She receives the beast's allegiance by surrendering something of her own, a distinct sign of her nature: "some poor thing you alone claim," as the second woman suggests. "The Dream," then, is an important poem, in part because it reveals Bogan's envisioning of the imaginative control of threatening psychological forces and prefigures the action and imagery of her later poems in which diffusion of the self, a form of "giving" of the self, occurs within a natural landscape and signals ultimate release.

Reviewing Bogan's poetry in 1941, Marianne Moore noted, "Anodynes are intolerable to her; she refuses to be deceived or self-deceived."[29] Moore's remark takes on increased meaning when we consider that Bogan was at points able to write poetry by imagining that the very act of writing might, at some moments, purge outdated, or outlived, structures of meaning and behavior. W. H. Auden's observations in 1942 about her poetry are especially perceptive in this context:

> It is only by reading and rereading that one comes to appreciate the steady growth of wisdom and technical mastery, the persistent eliminations of the consolations of stoicism and every other kind of poetic theatre, the achievement of an objectivity about personal experience which is sought by many but found only by the few who dare face the Furies.[30]

Such "persistent elimination" of artificial effects, a further purifying of her customary gestures, characterizes the new poems of *Poems and New Poems*. In his review of the book Malcolm Cowley wrote that Bogan's true subject "was always poetry itself"[31] and Stanley Kunitz, moved toward contemplating a fabular connection, asserted that the book revealed that Bogan's "true world . . . is 'the sunk land of dust and flame,' where an unknown terror is king, presiding over the fable of a life, in the deep night swarming with images of reproach and desire."[32]

In 1939 Bogan laid out essential considerations about the woman artist's quest for poetic development as she ages. The female poet, she suggests, must eliminate some earlier postures of rebellion—postures that youth more rightly assumes—against natural laws of aging and mortality.

> It is difficult to say what a woman poet should concern herself with as she grows older, because women poets who have produced an impressively bulky body of work are few. But is there any reason to believe that a woman's spiritual fibre is less sturdy than a man's? Is it not possible for a woman to come to terms with herself if not with the world; to withdraw more and more, as times goes on, her own personality from her productions; to stop childish fears of death and eschew charming rebellions against facts?[33]

The quotation comes from Bogan's review of Edna St. Vincent Millay's *Huntsman, What Quarry?*, and the questions are surely loaded. A woman must accept herself and not "the world," Bogan resolves. Clearly, she saw a culture that sought to arrest women's development. The great temptation for the female lyric poet would be to engage in a youthful "cry" long after youth had departed—as if women in particular were suspect if they assumed the dignified voice of maturity and attempted to write poems of greatness in their middle and later life. While she had admired Millay's earlier work, she found her contemporary in the book under review to be resisting maturity, and her questions urge Millay and other women poets to grow more serious as artists as they mature and thus to resist public expectations. The general public was too easily satisfied with its poets, particularly its female poets, whose psychological development was delayed. And in a manner somewhat like that which T. S. Eliot prescribed in "Tradition and the Individual Talent," she would urge the mature poet to withdraw the more limited aspects of "personality" from her poems.

After the publication of *Poems and New Poems* Bogan employed two principal visual emphases that reflect her maturing poetic: images of transparency and liquidity; and images of bodily dissolution. She brings to her poetry a new focus on the refinement of experience. As in her poem "The Dragonfly" (1963), a transparency of image is repeated frequently; like the dragonfly, the poem illusorily may seem "made of almost nothing" (*BE* 123), posing as a brilliantly lightened second self. She recoils from engaging in contests over past incident. Like the "tendril of convolvulus" in "Morning," she too "Succeeds in avoiding / All but the smaller thorns," by creating an "ascending spiral" toward release from obsession (*BE* 131).

In a 1959 journal entry, Bogan wrote revealingly of her emphatic desire to forgo the psyche's needless suffering:

> The thing to thank God for (I said, looking down at the counter, heaped with small, vivid objects) is the presence of the sunlight and the absence of mental anguish (in which I lived, like a fish in jelly, for so long). It was a heavy pain within the heart; like a voice, it prompted incidence and evil, within the ear. It was like a dreadful fire lit by chance—an undermining fire bred by pressure—self-fed, self-engendered. . . . (*JAR* 166)

Her meditation, prompted it would seem, by the sight of "small, vivid objects" may cause us to recall her admiration of Rilke, whose "object poems" inspired and perhaps comforted her. She had "discovered" him in 1935 while writing *The Sleeping Fury*. His poetry, she wrote to Theodore Roethke, "is carved out of agony, just as a statue is carved out of marble." Roethke himself, she advised, should further sharpen his perceptions so that he might deepen his work as Rilke had. "And you must let yourself suffer, once in a while, lovey, in order that you may do same."[34] It was

Rilke's ability to surrender himself to objects of contemplation that she particularly admired and that she sought to emulate. By 1948 she was faulting Yeats for an inability to surrender to the universal processes of aging and mortality. "I think that Yeats tends to bore us, now that we are ripe and mature, because Yeats, unlike all the other poets of his stature, refused *to give in, to flow*. . . . Lawrence and Rilke and Mallarmé *flowed*. . . ."[35]

Her tentative attempt to engage in self-surrender, a widening of poetic horizons beyond the ego, became more visible in *The Collected Poems*. The repetitive chant of "Train Tune" evinces a number of her central images, now simplified and reiterated. In this series of phrases we pass *through* most phenomenon but *along* love, which may neither be penetrated nor possessed:

> Back through plains
> Back through flowers
> Back through birds
> Back through rain
>
> Back through smoke
> Back through noon
> Back along love
> Back through midnight.
>
> (*BE* 118)

The more ambitious "After the Persian" portrays a fluent and translucent self. In 1937 Bogan wrote to Roethke, "My aim is to sound so pure and so liquid that travelers will take me across the desert with them."[36] In "After the Persian" she achieves much of that fluidity of effect. As Frank informs us, the poem is in part influenced by Bogan's response to Persian miniatures that she enjoyed contemplating for their delicate formal qualities at the Boston Museum of Fine Art and the Metropolitan Museum of Art in New York.[37] Her speaker opens with a quiet refusal of obsession and thralldom, transforming earlier preoccupations as she imagines inhabiting an environment beyond obsession. The setting is no longer a sealed room or a burning tropical landscape. Bogan emphasizes, in part through repetitions of the word *here,* that her work involves imagining a new topography for freed energies. A "terrible jungle" of infertility and illusion is rejected precisely because she had correctly judged its false attractions earlier. Any state of being that she knows to be sterile and deceptive must be withstood:

> I do not wish to know
> The depths of your terrible jungle:

> From what nest your leopard leaps
> Or what sterile lianas are at once your
> serpents' disguise and home.

(*BE* 115)

She imagines a threshold of plenitude in which living beings are not hardened into facile artifice or static conception. In this paradisal landscape of the psyche, creatures engage in continual flux, and Bogan renders an uncategorizable state of being through jewel-like lines. Moving from the wilderness of the youthful quester to the garden of mature knowledge, her speaker triumphs over fruitless obsession:

> Here the moths take flight at evening;
> Here at morning the dove whistles and the pigeons coo.
> Here, as night comes on, the fireflies wink and snap
> Close to the cool ground,
> Shining in a profusion
> Celestial or marine.

(*BE* 115)

In the poem's second section, Bogan provides an imagistic retrospective, concluding, "I know what winter brings." A symbolic hunt follows in which, significantly, the speaker does not participate. The "trophies" of the hunters must simply "bleed and perish." Yet the landscape that the speaker inhabits remains fresh and cooling:

> They will bring the trophies home
> To bleed and perish
> Beside the trellis and the lattices,
> Beside the fountain, still flinging diamond water,
> Beside the pool
> (Which is eight-sided, like my heart).

(*BE* 116)

In a gloss on one of her most puzzling images, Bogan informed May Sarton that "the eight-sided heart" symbolizes freedom: "Love of things, I suppose, more than love of human beings. . . . The delight of the collector. . . . The delight of the naturalist . . . ; the delight of the amateur in the arts. . . ."[38] While the singular heart is self-mirroring and narrow, the "eight-sided heart" is the heart of developed being, for if the heart is to be released from obsessive suffering, it must open to renewed and various experience.

Tellingly, in one of her notebooks from 1935, Bogan records her deep suspicions of the torturous course of romantic attachment. She castigates herself for earlier being guilty of "non-identity" as one of the "self-murderous Fools of love-love-love." The price for such romantic delusion proves to be "endless torture, endless *self*-betrayal."[39] Yet in a late journal entry she made a further distinction: "[T]he poems depended on the *ability* to love. (Yeats kept saying this, to the end.) The *faculty* of loving. A talent. A gift" (*JAR* 172-73). "After the Persian" is in some senses an imagistic contemplation of artful and natural form that refers to one aspect of her own giftedness, that is, to her *faculty* for love as it may, nevertheless, evade self-betrayal and sinister attachment.

Without ligature, the poem's free verse sections suggest a widening of boundaries that may press love outward and beyond the narcissistic ego. The first section establishes a benevolent site; the next reviews the past; the third honors the "treasure" of poetry itself; the fourth contrasts present fulfillment with past suffering; the fifth enacts departure. With each section Bogan extends into further imagistic dimensions, presenting stages toward release. Similarly, "the shimmer of evil" is replaced by "the shell's iridescence / And the wild bird's wing." Both the iridescent shell and "the crystal" that would "clasp" reality indicate her new sense of form to be as "Weightless as amber, / Translucent as the currant on the branch, / Dark as the rose's thorn" (116). The self must recede from the poem, to be supplanted by its natural surroundings. In her focus on weightless movement and fluctuating imagery, Bogan drafts the gradual evaporation of self-as-poem and poem-as-self:

> Goodbye, goodbye!
> There was so much to love, I could not love it all;
> I could not love it enough.
>
> Some things I overlooked, and some I could not find.
> Let the crystal clasp them
> When you drink your wine, in autumn.
>
> (*BE* 117)

Just as the "treasure" of experience rendered into poetry must prove "weightless," so too the speaker must become a disembodied spirit freed of even so much as linguistic confines. In "After the Persian" Bogan both honors her previous work and expresses her ability to move beyond former stylistic and thematic preoccupations. By establishing a sphere of plenitude and surplus ("There was so much to love, I could not love it all") she passes her desires on to the reader and announces her own departure as the poem ends.

Bogan sheds light on her processes in a review of Auden's *Collected Poems*: "A moment occurs (or should occur) when the growing artist is able to bequeath his tricks to his imitators. The mature writer rejects the treasured 'originality' and the darling virtuosities of his apprenticeship in art, as well as the showy sorrows and joys of his apprenticeship to life, often just in time."[40] "After the Persian" confirms her establishment of a newly pliable and fluent line that supplants some of her earlier stylistic strategies.

From the middle 1930s until her death in 1970 Bogan lived alone (or occasionally with her daughter). Her solitude marks her later work. Her progress as a poet was accompanied without a philosophical or religious system to sustain her, as she was already proud to mention to a correspondent in 1935: "The reconciliation of the warring elements in my own nature was effected in such an unconscious and unknowable Jungian manner that I have become rather impatient with surrogates for religion, and life-lines and rocks of ages and snug harbors and other dogmatic frameworks."[41] This attitude of self-reliance is reflected in the draft of her unpublished poem "Letter to Mrs. Q's Sister" in which she glances at betrayal and particularly at adultery but closes with an image of peace, that of a woman aware of her own inner and outer riches: "O what woman should weep, because of this, / Safe with her dove, her fountain, her earth, her ilex?"[42] Surely whatever periods of serenity Bogan experienced had been earned despite adversity, and the late poems chart her deepening sense of at least the temporary rewards of her continuing struggles. Laboriously, and despite her own physical and psychological periods of illness, Bogan in her last poems attempted to dissolve obsessive content in favor of the dramatization of a sensibility that had confronted and relinquished obsession.

"Song for the Last Act," written in 1948 and inspired by Bogan's meeting in the same year with T. S. Eliot,[43] may offer more complex cues for considering poetic and psychic release in her later poems. In "Song for the Last Act" Bogan pays homage not only to Eliot as a mature artist and, in a sense, to the ideals of high modernism, but to her own longevity as a self-conscious artist. She was justifiably proud of the poem, writing to Humphries: "[A]t least one more poetic work will be published, proving that *women* can carry on to some slight degree, *in* their 50's."[44] Devoted to the "unprinted silence," the poem progressively charts the psychological necessity (and expense) of composition. As in "After the Persian," translucent imagery dominates. And yet here the poet explicitly describes censors: the archetypal others figured in marble and lead, the recalcitrance of language itself, and the costly expenditures of the poet's psyche. From the artist's "frame" to the page of poetry, to the living scene, Bogan examines the act of wresting the poem from heterogeneous and resistant materials.

The poem encloses many of Bogan's primary themes, reconstituting the repression of energy and stalled time ("another summer loath to go") and making silence the weft of composition as "the staves are shuttled over with a stark / Unprinted silence" (*BE* 119). In her emphasis on stasis and the "rust of time and desire" after a completed voyage, she returns to the territory of "A Tale."

The poem's form is complex; each of three eight-line stanzas with its envelope rhymes is followed by an isolated line that repeats in full the first line of the stanza preceding it. The tone is elegiac, and yet while Bogan focuses on "the last act," the accumulated meaning of a life, its images do not foreclose upon one another. The poem repeatedly refers to visual acts—looking, reading, and seeing—but in each instance we are to view a symbolic scene beyond the template of vision. The ritualistic surroundings of the first stanza are described as "darkening" despite the bright thrusts of color in melon "yellow as young flame" and "quilled dahlias." The stanza conveys a friezelike quality even as the lead and marble figures in this dark pastoral are seemingly daemonic and engaged in their own visual pastime, for they "watch the show." These apparitions attending art predict the poet's mortality, figured by hanging scythes:

> Where quince and melon, yellow as young flame,
> Lie with quilled dahlias and the shepherd's crook.
> Beyond, a garden. There, in insolent ease
> The lead and marble figures watch the show
> Of yet another summer loath to go
> Although the scythes hang in the apple trees.
>
> (*BE* 119)

In the second full stanza, devoted to the ear, the music of poetry proves uncontrollable. The poet must meet high flux to make meaning: "In a double dream / I must spell out the storm, the running stream. / The beat's too swift. The notes shift in the dark" (119). The poem is itself the "double dream" that distills the "storm" of experience and allows the poet to internalize the other, or to have him at "heart." The words that the speaker reads on the page "shake and bleed" and are thus given the fleshly qualities that were absent from the first stanza's announced, but immediately frustrated, contemplation of a human face.

In the final full stanza Bogan examines the outcome of knowing another's "heart": a weight of barbarity, of human life delivered to tragic purposes:

> The rigging and the cargo and the slaves
> On a strange beach under a broken sky.
> O not departure, but a voyage done!
> The bales stand on the stone; the anchor weeps
> Its red rust downward, and the long vine creeps
> Beside the salt herb, in the lengthening sun.
>
> Now that I have your heart by heart, I see.

(BE 119–20)

Action is reduced finally to that of a portentous "long vine" that "creeps." The scene is the inverse of "After the Persian," for here the environment portrays human misery accompanying daemonic mystery. "Wharves with their great ships and architraves" signify a completed voyage that is marked by adversity and anguish. The poem's isolated single lines move from "I look" to "I read," to "I see," the final verb widening meaning in this context to suggest gathering comprehension. Similarly, in the poem's progression of stanzas, Bogan moves from the artist's face to the voice, and then to the heart, internalizing the development of meaning.

It is important that Bogan wrote often of the body—bodily appetites, bodily knowledge, bodily resistance to inchoate or complexly organized coercion. Yet in her late poems the body is diffused, made benignly strange, at times a source of symbol in retrospect. In "Song for the Last Act" she effects an internalizing of a body from the face to the voice and the heart, suggesting that hers is a willing effort to remember and to experience, "to have by heart." Yet here I would like to emphasize that it is not the actual face of the other that is seen but the surrounding frame, not the actual voice but the words on a page—words that assume the quality of music but in their symbolic evocation exceed musical form. The final eight-line stanza of "Song for the Last Act" depicts a completed voyage of suffering in which the red rust of the anchor (linked to the heart that is petrified by past trauma) and the salted herb (surely suggestive of the "labor of tears" in so many of her poems) point to the body in coded form. In much earlier poetry images of the body take on a palpable, nearly tactile quality. They are embedded into the poems in ways that allow us to contemplate the actual body as much as its symbolic associations. After *The Sleeping Fury*, however, the body would seem rarefied, images of it appearing to be nearly transparent. In "The Dragonfly," for instance, the insect's body is "made of almost nothing / But of enough / To be great eyes / And diaphanous double vans" (*BE* 123). The body that she chooses to describe is translucent and finally a "husk," emptied out by having fully spent itself in its environment and through the short span of its allotted lifetime. In "The Sorcerer's Daughter" a young woman possesses her self-knowledge initially by viewing a scar on her thumb, the scar indicating meaning beyond itself, as if the body's scars determine destiny. Bogan might very well have agreed with Moore's estimate in a review of Bogan's poetry: "[T]he scar is a credential."[45] This emphasis on the body as it may be "read" for meaning is even more clear in "Cartography," published in 1938, in which veins and a "gaunt hand" reveal

> The wiry brand
> Of the life we bear
>
> Mapped like the great
> Rivers that rise
> Beyond our fate
> And distant from our eyes.
>
> (*BE* 107)

The body here signifies a larger life than an individual's, for the poem broadens toward forces of nature and spirituality. The body is, in a sense, "branded" in a way that allows us to intuit unaccountable and mysterious events, a larger design beyond human ratiocination. In "After the Persian" Bogan imagines a paradisal environment in which the body, steeped with light, is somehow akin to light: "[T]he day stains with what seems to be more than the sun / What may be more than my flesh" (*BE* 115).

In this context, two early poems that Bogan chose to withhold from later collections may allow us to extend our responses. These two poems show her early attempts at enacting release and simultaneously forecast her more mature strategies. Her refusal to reprint these poems may have been predicated upon her sense of their psychological immaturity. "A Letter," first published in *Body of This Death* (5–7), records a journey toward silence. The poem displays less of the finished quality of much of Bogan's work, which may account in part for her distrust of it. Nevertheless, it depicts a memorable landscape in which a woman attempts to fulfill inchoate longings. The poem begins at the end of autumn: "I came here, being stricken, stumbling out / At last from streets." Under "a cracked and fluent heaven," in an atmosphere of dissociation, the speaker struggles beneath boughs "like roots" that "strike into the sky" (5). Within the upended universe of the poem, the traveler is acutely aware of her mortality, "the goal a coffer of dust." Pointedly, this is "the journey to nothing or any desire." As the body is arrested, sensuality proves a false promise:

> To feel my body as arid, as safe as a twig
> Broken away from whatever growth could snare it
> Up to a spring, or hold it softly in summer
> Or beat it under in snow.

Halfway through the poem, Bogan uncharacteristically puts forward an explicit statement: "I must get well" (6). To get well in the context of the poem is to *feel* again. The battle to experience emotions animates these poems of a frozen psyche. Yet from a stated desire for committed and fluent feeling, the poet arrives at negation. Opposites cancel one another: "To escape is nothing. Not to escape is nothing" (6). The final line with its superficial tone of disillusion and self-deprecation ("And now I have written you this, it is nothing") completes this "journey to nothing." Paradoxically, the assertion of journey's end amounts to a victory of sorts. If "beauty is nothing," the poem as another "nothing" achieves its own peculiar beauty, and the traveler presents the other with no less than a well-made and resounding "nothing" uncannily managed through destructive energy.

"Words for Departure" (*BTD* 10–11) similarly may complicate our discussion, for the word "nothing" is once again foregrounded, and likewise a traveler must take instructions. First published in *Measure* in 1921, the poem opens with paralyzing oppositions: "Nothing was remembered, nothing forgotten." Within this internalized landscape, as in "Medusa," Bogan's figures appear stalled. The poem closes with what is a prescription both for taking leave of a lover and for assuming authority in poetry, particularly in poetry in which words must be fitfully reclaimed from silence:

> But at the end, be insolent;
> Be absurd—strike the thing short off;
> Be mad—only do not let talk
> Wear the bloom from silence.
>
> And go away without fire or lantern.
> Let there be some uncertainty about your departure.
>
> (*BTD* 11)

Her early caution ("let there be some uncertainty about your departure") conditions her last poems of release. In much later work, departure is the task of a lyric speaker who moves quietly beyond the frame of limited human understanding to become a force aligned to nature and yet seemingly without corporeal limitations.

I have brought these two early poems into a discussion of Bogan's late work as evidence of the coherence and consistency of her vision. As a young poet in her projected "journey to nothing" she anticipated her last strategies. Although she was to abandon the earlier poems' tones of contention, in her final poems she presented a self that ultimately had to be liberated from inherited forms of relationship. In the early poems she prematurely grasped at a form of wisdom that must later have seemed, given her critical rigor, suspiciously unearned. When recast from the mature perspective that she would develop, her theme was intimated with conviction and complexity. The "nothing" of withheld context dilated into her contemplation of silence and mortality in later work.

Bogan's final collection, *The Blue Estuaries*, remains the definitive collection of her work. It contains the 105 poems upon which she staked her reputation, poems of technical excellence and, often, psychological complexity.

In the new poems collected in this final anthology of her work, Bogan increasingly honed a transparent self in language and invested in a search for symbolic messages. Such poetry reveals a completion of the processes that we have studied. In place of resistance, she progressively casts images of curious luminosity and moments of unexpected release. Her last poems contain references to silence, and yet they oppose the worst effects of silence by making, through the efforts of a meticulous and exacting sensibility, "treasure / Weightless as amber." Her course in poetry is markedly similar to that detailed in her own description of Emily Dickinson's progression: "[A]s her life goes on, everything becomes whittled down, evanescent. Her handwriting becomes a kind of fluid print; her poems become notations; all seems to be on the point of disappearing. And suddenly all disappears."[46] The release from obsession, in particular, was the primary act of Bogan's later poems. She projected a new tonal range that prompted William Meredith to review the book as "a feat of character"[47] and William Heyen to refer to the collection as "a cold, comforting book."[48] If she had been unable to write much poetry during her later years, her contemplations of release made possible her temporary moments of fluency, and the "blue estuaries" of her poems present receptivity transformed into reflection and renewal.

In "Night," first printed in *Poetry* in 1962, Bogan suggests that just as the river's current meets the sea's tide, so too the conscious mind must meet the unconscious mind through the medium of the poem. Aligning her speaker with the natural world, she acknowledges all that "moves" beyond the isolated self:

> The cold remote islands
> And the blue estuaries
> Where what breathes, breathes
> The restless wind of the inlets,
> And what drinks, drinks
> The incoming tide;
>
> Where shell and weed
> Wait upon the salt wash of the sea,
> And the clear nights of stars
> Swing their lights westward
> To set behind the land;
>
> Where the pulse clinging to the rocks
> Renews itself forever;
> Where, again on cloudless nights,
> The water reflects
> The firmament's partial setting;
>
> —O remember
> In your narrowing dark hours
> That more things move
> Than blood in the heart.

(*BE* 130)

Surely, "Night" is a signature poem of her late work, for the implosive themes of her earlier poetry are supplanted by images of renewal and often benign and mysterious correspondence. And it is from this poem that Bogan derived the title of her final book of poems. Here the faculty of memory, so often a mixed capacity in Bogan's poems, is poised for release beyond selfhood: the final stanza's opening imperative "—O remember" calls for memory that may move further than the individual's past, beyond "blood in the heart" to the larger rhythms of life. The poem's repetition of *s* sounds in its twenty lines and its narrow vocabulary of central images contribute to its coherence and resonance. Self-renewal is achieved through meditation on the outer natural world, and through contemplation of poetry as an art that transforms the sea of the unconscious beyond romance or neurosis. The "blood in the heart" that we may recall as volatile within that brilliantly cold poem of repression, "Winter Swan," is now propelled toward "the firmament."

Notably, those of Bogan's poems that were composed despite prolonged periods in which she did not write poetry register her desire for purifying detachment. A central poem in this undertaking is "The Meeting," in which she reexamines her connection to a subconscious archetype that defuses the will. Neither resistance nor recognition defeats this censor, but a requestioning of identity allows speech to occur. Written around 1956 and published in February 1957 in the *New Yorker*, "The Meeting" presents an experience of self-impediment. Bogan initially conceived of the poem's central character as her second husband, writing to John Hall Wheelock in 1956: "It certainly is the record of a recurring subconscious experience, concerning which I used to suffer a good deal; but now I am only curious and puzzled."[49] And in March of the same year she wrote to Glenway Wescott: "It came out practically whole, although a few shifts had to be made. The change in the dream-creature's personality had taken place. . . ."[50] This "dream-creature" falters rather than holds the speaker's gaze:

> Each time I found him, it was always the same:
> Recognition and surprise,
> And then the silence, after the first words,
> And the shifting of the eyes.
>
> Then the moment when he had nothing to say
> And only smiled again,
> But this time toward a place beyond me,
>   where I could not stay—
> No world of men.

As Bogan's similes suggest, the speaker and censor exist within a close relationship; indeed, they share kinship. Yet the other is not so much a failed love object as a transformed embodiment of whatever psychic force inhibits creative fulfillment. The speaker recognizes the other as a function of her own apparatus, present "at the deepest bottom of the dream."

> Eye to eye we look, and we greet each other
> Like friends from the same land.
> Bitter compliance! Like a faithless brother
> You take and drop my hand.
>
>   (*BE* 129)

That such a figure must both "take *and* drop" (emphasis mine) the speaker's hand reflects the unsatisfactory nature of the writing encounter. The transaction ends in silence and withdrawal. In the final image of the dropped hand we may nevertheless detect an ambiguous note of release. Now that the other can no longer be locked in place within one nefarious identity, the speaker may be freed to redirect her energies and to question her previously calcified understanding of the past. What is worth special notice is the speaker's recognition of error in her earlier too-ready allotment of identity and intent. The identity of the other, after all, is at the heart of the poem. Is this an animus figure, the "broken will" that will emerge in "Psychiatrist's Song"? If so, it proves a figure of weakness and failed resolve, for this vacillating man deflects forceful completion. At the same time, the "faithless brother" who is discovered "at the bottom of the dream" in "The Meeting" would seem to be an image of her own obsession, as a line in a letter using similar language suggests. As we recall, in writing to Sarton about "After the Persian," Bogan refers to her pleasure in "objects, both natural and artificial," a pleasure that developed "ever since the *obsessive* person [that she had been] was left behind (or buried, if you like, in the lowest layer of the dream)."[51] "The Meeting," then, suggests that "the faithless brother" is obsession itself as it may circumscribe achievement and fulfillment.

In *The Blue Estuaries* Bogan included a number of poems written earlier and later retrieved and revised. Elements of a fixed fate underlie these poems. Speech may be bound and silenced within a talisman, a symbol that, as Bogan conceived it, projects her speaker's fortune. It would seem that her decision to revive previously abandoned poems was not arbitrary but reflected her commitment to viewing experience itself as a possession that may be retrieved and "read" as symbols are read. Such retrieved poems indicate her new ability to countenance projections of fate. If earlier such poems had seemed negligible, over time and through revision they assumed proper status as portents and could themselves be released for publication. The charmlike poems were anticipated in *Dark Summer* by "Old Countryside" (*BE* 52) in which the final disturbing image resembles an engraving that may be read to warn of tragedy. As we had seen in "The Mark" (*BE* 38), the past survives within the unconscious and there creates its own "epoch" outside of chronological time. Similarly, in the late retrieved poems "July Dawn" and "March Twilight" signs prove inauspicious and sinister. To read the charm is to seek both knowledge of the past and, simultaneously, to control the effects of the past on the present by possessing a portent.

In the retrieved poem "The Sorcerer's Daughter" (*BE* 125)—twenty years old before it was revised and revived—ill fortune allows a daughter to recognize herself and her past, providing her with a narrative, however bitter, of identity. The fatalism that the sorcerer's daughter exhibits is, at last, a proclamation of self-knowledge. The speaker is a daughter, point-edly, a child of magic who takes on her father's beliefs in talismans as her own:

> But this series of events had no good augeries about it:
>   no birds flew into fortunate quarters
> When the knock came upon the door. Matter did not creak or
>   space mutter.
> Nothing fell up or down; the weather did not give it much
>   help,
> And time and place were always wrong.
>
> It was crossed from the start
> With all the marks of luck changing
> From better to worse.
> And by these tokens I begin to think it is mine.
>
> <div align="right">(<i>BE</i> 125)</div>

The sorcerer's daughter acknowledges the tragic contours of her life in the poem's catalog of signs; she is now less possessed than possessor as she concludes of her past, "It is mine."

Written in 1959 and appended to the previous poem, "The Young Mage" presents a series of encouragements and cautions as if to complicate initial perceptions of fatalism, for now watchfulness, a canniness about signs, is encouraged. Notes on the virtues of independence, pleasure, and tenacity are followed by cryptic warnings:

> And he said: Hold
> Fast to the leaves' silver
> And the flowers' gold.
>
> And he said: Beware
> Of the round web swinging from the angle
> Of the steep stair,
> And of the comet's hair.
>
> <div align="right">(<i>BE</i> 126)</div>

The magus's admonitions point to the hard labor inherent in uniting spirit and body—and to the hair-thin, almost invisible impediments to good fortune.

Bogan concludes *The Blue Estuaries* with three poems that recapitu-late a number of the crises to which her body of work in varied proportions attends, including violent rupture between self and other and recognition of the unconscious as the daemonic.

The first two "songs" of "Three Songs" were written in 1966 and 1967. The final poem, "Masked Woman's Song," was characterized by Bogan as "a fairly old erotic song."[52] Nevertheless she regarded it when retrieved as belonging to the same field "of dream and aberration" as the later poems.[53] All the poems in the triptych are identified as songs, for Bogan here invested in an emphatically rhythmic line, choosing to wed psychological exploration with the tradition of the lyric song. "Three Songs" concludes Bogan's final volume of collected poems, voicing a newly emerged portion of the unconscious ("Little Lobelia's Song"); acknowledging early psychological wounds and imagining serene release ("Psychiatrist's Song"); and recognizing the effects of obsession ("Masked Woman's Song").

In the previous chapter I discussed "Little Lobelia's Song" as a manifestation of preoedipal experience. In the context of the late poetry, this poem profitably may also be read in terms of separation into a split self. We might recall that a note at the top of a draft indicates that the poem dramatizes "'an autonomous complex,'" for an unintegrated portion of the psyche is released into speech. The poem was written when Bogan was sixty-nine and continuing at that date—four years before her death—to emancipate herself from the obsessive materials of her early past. Ruth Limmer, speculating on the poem's source, provocatively asks, "[M]ight it not be the voice that was never permitted to speak in public and was hardly ever allowed to utter even in private?"[54] It would seem that the child of the unconscious haunts the adult. Yet Little Lobelia asserts both her vulnerability and her power:

> Not lost but abandoned,
> Left behind;
> This is my hand
> Upon your mind.

(*BE* 132)

Whether a buried child of the psyche or, as Bowles convincingly argues, a "voice" not only from the past but a partial manifestation of the side effects of Bogan's prescribed doses of Librium,[55] the poet has transformed this phantom into art. The child voice that had been "Not lost but abandoned, / Left behind" must now be heard. No longer repressed, Lobelia is free to "become the poem":

> You look at your face
> In the looking glass.

> This is the face
> My likeness has.
>
> Give me back your sleep
> Until you die,
> Else I weep, weep,
> Else I cry, cry.
>
> (*BE* 132–33)

The child within the psyche cannot understand her situation. She can only utter her indelible sorrow. Bogan posits the memory of childhood in her journal as similarly uneffaced:

> The child lives in a region it knows nothing about. So that whatever memory of childhood remains is stable and perfect. *It cannot be judged and it can never disappear* [emphasis mine]. Memory has it inexplicably, and will have it forever. These things have been actually "learned by heart." (*JAR* 101)

Like the child-self, Little Lobelia survives in a solution of unmediated, plaintive expression.

Bogan suggests the sources from which Lobelia emerges and alludes to the secret origins of psychological affliction in the second of her three songs, "Psychiatrist's Song." In the poem, psychiatrist and patient meld into one being, journeying toward "vision" rather than remaining within the boundaries of the talking cure.

> Those
> Concerning whom they have never spoken and
>   thought never to speak;
> That place
> Hidden, preserved,
> That even the exquisite eye of the soul
> Cannot completely see.
> But they are there:
> Those people, and that house, and that evening, seen
> Newly above the dividing window-sash—
> The young will broken
> And all time to endure.
>
> (*BE* 134)

Although undetectable to psychiatrist and patient, the people of the past and the setting in which their actions took place are inscribed in the unconscious.

The psychiatrist's position particularly interests Bogan, for (like the poet in this instance) the psychiatrist must investigate an individual's early history, probing the origin of present suffering. The psychiatrist and patient search together for the psychic antechamber in which the past has been preserved and in response to which current symptoms of psychological suffering arise. The patient and psychiatrist embark upon a journey toward art itself and its own species of "aberration":

> I hear.
> But far away are the mango trees (*the mangrove*
> *swamps, the mandrake root . . .*)
> And the thickets of—are they palms?
> I watch them as though at the edge of sleep.
> I often journey toward them in a boat without oars,
> Trusting to rudder and sail.
>
> (*BE* 134)

Moving from the mango fruits to the mangrove swamps and to the mandrake root, the associations shift from the benign to the dangerously entwining and sinking land of the swamp, to the narcotic of the mandrake, a member of the nightshade family. This slide in meaning is effected through close linguistic similarities; surely the syllable *man* beginning each word not only calls up associations with specifically male threats, as many of her readers note, but with the generic human propensity to inscribe form with nightmarish associations. Yet at last this speaker enters a realm of strange peace willingly and without paralysis. The poem's concluding stanzas, echoing the farewell of "After the Persian," allow a beneficent silence to defeat the throngs of past voices and the source of original trauma. Without engaging in an act of will, the speaker enters an imaginative vision that delivers her from her own demons:

> And I am on firm dry land, with, closely waiting,
> A hill all sifted over with shade
> Wherein the silence waits.
>
> Farewell, phantoms of flesh and of ocean!
> Vision of earth
> Heal and receive me.
>
> (*BE* 135)

The journey's conclusion may appear ambiguous, for the psychiatrist/ patient may be seen as escaping private turmoil simply to withdraw into nature, a conclusion reached by several of Bogan's critics. Yet, I would argue, Bogan's conclusion is far more resonant and assumes transport toward poetry itself. We see here the repressed that must "become the poem" as Bogan enacts processes that make composition possible: "I often journey . . . in a boat without oars, / Trusting to rudder and sail" (134). Trusting both to the unconscious (the boat without oars) and to craft (rudder and sail), she may compose the poem. Poetry, which must be "endured," may also heal. The "life-saving process" that began for Bogan as a fourteen-year-old girl who had discovered she was a poet continued in old age. Rather than the earth alone, it is finally a "vision of earth"—the very act of envisioning through poetry—that may "heal and save." She imagines a journey in which silence itself must speak through the poem, for the past is not so much transcended (here it exists independently and cannot be destroyed); rather, it is departed from for a "*vision* of earth," a new imagining of the natural, that may grant at least temporary serenity.

The Blue Estuaries concludes with a riddling poem that suggests another sort of arrival. The third song in this grouping, "Masked Woman's Song," dramatizes obsession. As Auden wrote in a review of Bogan's work, "Self-development is a process of self-surrender, for it is the Self that demands the exclusive attention of all experiences, but offers none in return."[56] Bogan decided to close the collection, her last, with an enigma of surrender: a poem that may be turned in many directions without our sensing that we have finally possessed it. In its evocation of a woman's past and in its status as a poem retrieved from the past, "Masked Woman's Song" doubly intimates closure. Through sight, a sense that, as we have seen, aroused conflicting responses from this poet, a woman has changed her moral bearings:

> Before I saw the tall man
> Few women should see,
> Beautiful and imposing
> Was marble to me.
>
> And virtue had its place
> And evil its alarms,
> But not for that worn face,
> And not in those roped arms.

(*BE* 136)

After meeting "the tall man / Few women should see," a woman's values are ravished. Once the woman encounters this man—whether animus, lover, or muse—virtue and evil are no longer in place.

The poem's imagistic argument remains deeply ambiguous. Does the masked woman experience beauty as classic, unchanging marble? Or is she at first unmoved by beauty; is it "marble" and thus cold to her? Do the images of a "worn face" and "roped arms" present us with a figure in struggle whose flesh has submitted to time? Or again, ambiguously, could the threatening tall man prove a figure of uncommon strength and living experience? Rather than the bound arms of a captive, might "roped arms" suggest sinewy muscle? In turn, could the tall man serve as an unconscious aspect of the woman, for her own face may be "worn," as a mask is worn, her own arms roped in bondage? The masked woman herself is doubly ambiguous as a figure whose disguise may heighten or diminish her power.

The poem's puzzling ambiguities place us in the same position as the masked woman; our own "vision" is obscured. What reading might we adopt? We would seem to be masked readers, puzzling our way through the multiple exposures of meaning in "Masked Woman's Song." As René Girard points out in another context, masks serve as monstrous doubles: "Masks stand at the equivocal frontier between the human and the 'divine,' between a differentiated order in the process of disintegration and its final undifferentiated state—the point where all differences, all monstrosities are concentrated, and from which a new order will emerge."[57] From behind her mask, Bogan's speaker narrates "a new order." Beauty and evil have abandoned their former places; the tall man as a figure of the monstrous has been at last recognized. As Cheryl Walker argues of the poem, "Bogan left it ambiguous intentionally, but if we read it as an expression in the forbidden-lover tradition [in women's poetry], we might interpret it as suggesting the deeply revolutionary consequences of indulging one's desire for power."[58] A poem written much earlier in Bogan's past, once abandoned and now recovered, "Masked Woman's Song" may suggest that suffering occurs through failed recognition of the power of the self and the other.

Both "The Changed Woman" (the poem that is one of this poet's earliest, already discussed in chapter 3) and "Masked Woman's Song" focus on the dynamism of moral awareness. They are not, surely, girls' songs, for here mature women suffer the aftereffects of their choices and are schooled in the distinctions between choice and compulsion. Both are aware of the seductive primacy of visual attraction, yet it is through the intensity of their power to respond to visual attractions that they are afforded the experience of creative trespass.

Significantly, one of Bogan's late preoccupations was the id. In 1969, a year before her death, she was attempting in prose to make further sense of unconscious energies. "The Id breaking through—(I have a new theory about outbreaks of the Id. The Id has no sex—did you know?")[59] She was beginning to write an essay for the *New Yorker* and noted, "I want to start off a piece with a mention of the *Id* rampant. But it's so hard to be definite about the *Id*. Impossible, in fact.—But I have a picture of it snorting like a dragon, and lashing its tail, like demons."[60] To explore the unconscious, to find for her time and culture a way to question meaning: these were obsessions from which she did not seek to withdraw. In her later poems she sought what she called in another context "the arts' progressive exploration and dissolution of binding reality."[61] In her allegiance to the lyric, the impassioned "cry," she expressed a desire to understand obsession, and she progressively sought to enact release from obsession, attempting to loosen the psychological constraints that determined, she found, both personal and cultural experience.

Bogan began her career with poems dramatizing revolt from a generalized emotional and social constriction, examining and rejecting cultural conceptions of romantic love. In her earlier agonistic poems, she enunciated a will to break from any constraining orders, figured as both within and outside the individual self. She began her career as the poet-alchemist whose experiments led her back to the flesh in the crucible as it defies reason and will. In her second book she explored self-consciously her own intimations about repression, figuring the unconscious as a site and attempting to explore the origins of psychic trauma. Later she would allude to recognition of the maternal, making a further accounting of one of the most vexing relationships of her life and identifying her own energies with maternal energies. Still later her poems pressed toward a new awareness of mortality and imagined a "vision" of earth as it may prompt an experience of psychological release. Her speakers sought a translucent sense of being and requestioned identity. Each poem was an experiment that suggested another narrative of arrival. Ultimately, her final poems envisioned a past as it now may be reread, renamed—and forgiven. Her eloquent final poems figured the release of all preoccupying constraints. Her allusions to secrecy and her deployment of the resonant image suggested to her a kind of power that most fully rendered her experience in its complexity. These habits, these achievements, allowed Louise Bogan to write poems that continue to resonate with charged energy and yet ultimately resist—as she would wish—our possession.

Notes

Introduction

1. Martha Collins, introduction to *Critical Essays on Louise Bogan* (Boston: G. K. Hall, 1984), p. 20.

2. Allen Tate, "R. P. Blackmur and Others," *Southern Review* 3 (Summer 1937): 191. Reprinted in Collins, *Critical Essays on Louise Bogan*, pp. 41–42.

3. Louis Untermeyer, "In a Gold Stain," *Saturday Review*, 1 Feb. 1930, 692. Reprinted in Collins, *Critical Essays on Louise Bogan*, p. 36.

4. Theodore Roethke, "The Poetry of Louise Bogan," in *On the Poet and His Craft: Selected Prose of Theodore Roethke*, Ralph J. Mills Jr. (Seattle: University of Washington Press, 1965), p. 134. Reprinted in Collins, *Critical Essays on Louise Bogan*, p. 87.

5. Gloria Bowles, *Louise Bogan's Aesthetic of Limitation* (Bloomington: Indiana University Press, 1987), p. 1.

6. Gwendolyn Sorrell Sell, "Louise Bogan: The Discipline of Recognition: Gender and Artistic Maturity" (diss., Emory University, 1988), p. 253.

7. Deborah Pope, *A Separate Vision: Isolation in Contemporary Women's Poetry* (Baton Rouge: Louisiana State University Press, 1984), p. 40.

8. Ibid., p. 52.

9. Ibid., p. 10.

10. Ibid., p. 52. I would like to point out that Jeanne Larsen takes the opposite view, arguing that "no one aspect seems more essential to our understanding of [Bogan's] art than its grounding in the body: the body that pulses, hears, and sings." "Lowell, Teasdale, Wylie, Millay and Bogan," in *The Columbia History of American Poets*, ed. Jay Parini and Brett C. Millier (New York: Columbia University Press, 1993), p. 231.

11. Patrick Moore, "Symbol, Mask, and Meter in the Poetry of Louise Bogan," in *Gender and Literary Voice*, ed. Janet Todd (New York: Holmes and Meier, 1980) p. 79.

12. Bowles, *Louise Bogan's Aesthetic of Limitation*, p. 2.

13. Mary K. DeShazer, *Inspiring Women: Reimagining the Muse* (New York: Pergamon Press, 1986), p. 46.

14. Kate Daniels, "The Demise of the 'Delicate Prisons': The Women's Movement in Twentieth-Century American Poetry," in *A Profile of Twentieth-Century American Poetry*, ed. Jack Myers and David Wojahn (Carbondale: Southern Illinois University Press, 1996), p. 242.

15. Allen Tate, "R. P. Blackmur," p. 192.

16. Yvor Winters, "The Poetry of Louise Bogan," *New Republic*, 16 Oct. 1929, 247. Reprinted in Collins, *Critical Essays on Louise Bogan*, p. 33.

17. Llewellyn Jones, *First Impressions: Essays on Poetry, Criticism, and Prosody* (New York: Books for Libraries, 1968), p. 118. Reprinted in Collins, *Critical Essays on Louise Bogan*, p. 27.

18. Léonie Adams, "'All Has Been Translated into Treasure,'" *Poetry* 85 (December 1954): 169. Reprinted in Collins, *Critical Essays on Louise Bogan*, p. 71.

19. Bowles, *Louise Bogan's Aesthetic of Limitation*, p. 1.

20. Elizabeth Dodd, *The Veiled Mirror and the Woman Poet: H.D., Louise Bogan, Elizabeth Bishop, and Louise Glück* (Columbia: University of Missouri Press, 1992), p. 74.

21. Bowles, *Louise Bogan's Aesthetic of Limitation*, pp. 51–52.

22. Suzanne Clark, *Sentimental Modernism: Women Writers and the Revolution of the Word* (Bloomington: Indiana University Press, 1991), p. 126.

23. Deborah Pope, "Music in the Granite Hill: The Poetry of Louise Bogan," in Collins, *Critical Essays on Louise Bogan*, p. 165.

24. Pope, *A Separate Vision*, p. 10.

25. Sandra M. Gilbert and Susan Gubar, eds., *Shakespeare's Sisters: Feminist Essays on Women Poets* (Bloomington: Indiana University Press, 1979), p. xxiii.

26. Paula Bennett, *My Life a Loaded Gun: Female Creativity and Feminist Poetics* (Boston: Beacon, 1986), p. 246.

27. Ibid., p. 247.

28. Ibid., p. 6.

29. Bogan to Sister M. Angela, 20 Aug. 1966, in *What the Woman Lived: Selected Letters of Louise Bogan, 1920–1970* (New York: Harcourt Brace, 1973), p. 368.

30. Bogan to Morton D. Zabel, 11 June 1937, in *What the Woman Lived*, p. 6n.

31. Louise Bogan, "The Situation in American Writing: Seven Questions," *Partisan Review* 6 (Fall 1939): 105. Reprinted in Collins, *Critical Essays on Louise Bogan*, p. 49.

32. Bogan, "Goethe," in *A Poet's Alphabet* (New York: McGraw-Hill, 1970), p. 201.

33. Ibid., p. 200.

34. Louise Bogan, "The Greatest Poet Writing in English Today," in *A Poet's Alphabet*, p. 456.

35. Louise Bogan, "Last Poems and Plays (1940)," in *A Poet's Alphabet*, p. 465.

36. Bogan, "Situation in American Writing," p. 105. Reprinted in Collins, *Critical Essays on Louise Bogan*, p. 49.

37. Bogan, "Emily Dickinson, The Poems," in *A Poet's Alphabet*, p. 94.

38. See ibid., pp. 88–103.

39. Babette Deutsch, *Poetry in Our Time* (New York: Columbia University Press, 1956), p. 239.

40. Jaqueline Ridgeway, *Louise Bogan* (Boston: Twayne, 1984), p. 13.

41. Louise Bogan, "The Heart and the Lyre," in *A Poet's Alphabet*, p. 428.

42. Ruth Lechlitner, "Mistress of Poetic Forms," *New York Herald Tribune Review of Books*, 30 May 1937, p. 2. Reprinted in Collins, *Critical Essays on Louise Bogan*, p. 43.

43. Morton D. Zabel, "The Flower of the Mind," *Poetry* 35 (December 1929): 160. Reprinted in Collins, *Critical Essays on Louise Bogan*, p. 35.

44. Bogan (addressee omitted),13 May 1944, in *What the Woman Lived*, p. 238.

45. Bogan, "Situation in American Writing," p. 107. Reprinted in Collins, *Critical Essays on Louise Bogan,* p. 52.

46. Ibid., p. 108.

47. Louise Bogan, "Formal Poetry," in *A Poet's Alphabet,* pp. 149–50.

48. Bowles, *Louise Bogan's Aesthetic of Limitation,* p. 35.

49. Louise Bogan, "Poetesses in the Parlor," *New Yorker* 12 (5 Dec. 1936): 45.

50. Ibid., pp. 48, 50.

51. Ibid., pp. 50, 52.

52. Ibid., p. 52.

53. Louise Bogan, *Achievement in American Poetry* (Chicago: Henry Regnery, 1951), pp. 22–23.

54. Ibid., p. 27.

55. Bogan to John Hall Wheelock, 1 July 1935, in *What the Woman Lived,* p. 86.

56. Bogan, "Virginia Woolf on Women," review of *A Room of One's Own, New Republic* 61 (18 December 1929): 105.

57. Bogan, "Heart and the Lyre," p. 426.

58. Ibid., p. 428.

59. Ibid., p. 429.

60. Ibid., p. 428.

61. Ibid., p. 429.

62. Ibid., p. 428.

63. Bogan, *Achievement in American Poetry,* p. 11.

64. See Elizabeth Frank, *Louise Bogan: A Portrait* (New York: Knopf, 1985), p. 49: "[S]he was then [in 1922] in psychiatric treatment with Dr. Samuel A. Tannenbaum, a Freudian who was known for his treatment of other writers in Bogan's sphere of acquaintance."

65. Bogan to John Hall Wheelock, 28 Oct. 1936, in *What the Woman Lived,* p. 138.

66. Sigmund Freud, "The Unconscious," in *The Standard Edition of the Complete Psychological Works of Sigmund Freud,* trans. James Strachey (London: Hogarth, 1978), 14:187.

67. Roethke, "Poetry of Louise Bogan," p. 138. Reprinted in Collins, *Critical Essays on Louise Bogan,* p. 90.

68. Bogan, *Achievement in American Poetry,* p. 23.

69. Although Rexroth complains bitterly of Bogan's lack of appreciation for Muriel Rukeyser's poetry, he believed Bogan to be a "militant feminist." Kenneth Rexroth, foreword to *The Poetic Vision of Muriel Rukeyser,* by Louise Kertesz (Baton Rouge: Louisiana State University Press, 1980), p. xiv.

Chapter 1. Violence and Difference: *Body of This Death*

1. Sara Via Pais, "Shapes of the Feminine Experience in Art," in *Women, the Arts, and the 1920s in Paris and New York,* ed. Kenneth W. Wheeler and Virginia Lee Lussier (New Brunswick, N.J.: Transaction Books, 1982), p. 50.

2. Frank, *Louise Bogan,* p. 71.

3. Pope, "Music in the Granite Hill," in Collins, *Critical Essays on Louise Bogan*, p. 157.

4. Louise Bogan, "James Joyce," in *A Poet's Alphabet*, p. 267.

5. Frank, *Louise Bogan*, p. 72.

6. Roethke, "Poetry of Louise Bogan," p. 138. Reprinted in Collins, *Critical Essays on Louise Bogan*, p. 90.

7. Carol Moldaw, "Form, Feeling, and Nature: Aspects of Harmony in the Poetry of Louise Bogan," in Collins, *Critical Essays on Louise Bogan*, p. 184.

8. Julia Kristeva, *Revolution in Poetic Language*, trans. Margaret Waller with an introduction by Leon S. Roudiez (New York: Columbia University Press, 1984), p. 16.

9. Frank, *Louise Bogan*, p. 113.

10. Cheryl Walker, *The Nightingale's Burden: Women Poets and Culture Before 1900* (Bloomington: Indiana University Press, 1982), p. 144.

11. Bogan to Ruth Benedict, 1 Dec. 1928. The poem led to a "mood of katharsis." See Bogan, *What the Woman Lived*, p. 39n.

12. Louise Bogan, "The Pleasures of Formal Poetry," in *A Poet's Alphabet*, pp. 151–52.

13. Pope, *A Separate Vision*, p. 18.

14. Ridgeway, *Louise Bogan*, p. 32.

15. Pope, *A Separate Vision*, p. 10.

16. Pope, "Music in the Granite Hill," in Collins, *Critical Essays on Louise Bogan*, p. 151.

17. Frank, *Louise Bogan*, p. 67.

18. Ronald Giles, "The Ironic Voice in Louise Bogan's 'Women'," *Poesis: A Journal of Criticism* 7, no. 5 (1987): p. 37.

19. Ibid., p. 40.

20. Ibid., p. 39.

21. See Frank, *Louise Bogan*, p. 364: "Generally speaking, [Bogan's] chief preoccupation is maturity: maturity in the artist, the art, the period, and the civilization at hand."

22. Mark Van Doren, review of *Body of This Death*, by Louise Bogan, *Nation*, 31 Oct. 1923, p. 494. Reprinted in Collins, *Critical Essays on Louise Bogan*, p. 29.

23. Jones, *First Impressions*, p. 118. Reprinted in Collins, *Critical Essays on Louise Bogan*, p. 27.

24. Bogan, "Situation in American Writing," p. 107. Reprinted in Collins, *Critical Essays on Louise Bogan*, p. 52.

25. Bogan to John Hall Wheelock, 28 July 1941, in *What the Woman Lived*, p. 222.

26. Bennett, *My Life a Loaded Gun*, pp. 265–66.

27. "Beginning of an Unpopular Song," in Louise Bogan Papers (Box 11, Folder 3), Special Collections Department, Amherst College Library.

28. "Letter to Mrs. Q's Sister," in Louise Bogan Papers (Box 11, Folder 43), Special Collections Department, Amherst College Library.

29. See Frank, *Louise Bogan*, p. 63.

30. "Hell," in Louise Bogan Papers (Box 11, Folder 19), Special Collections Department, Amherst College Library.

31. Bogan to Morton D. Zabel, 4 Dec. 1936, in *What the Woman Lived*, p. 145.

32. Bogan to May Sarton, 16 Feb. 1954, in *What the Woman Lived*, p. 284.

33. Adrienne Rich, back cover blurb for *The Blue Estuaries: Poems, 1923–1968* (New York: Ecco, 1988).

CHAPTER 2. REPRESSION AND SECRECY: *DARK SUMMER*

1. Sigmund Freud, "Repression," in *The Standard Edition of the Complete Psychological Works,* 14:147.

2. Frank, *Louise Bogan,* p. 108.

3. Hélène Cixous, "The Laugh of the Medusa," trans. Keith Cohen and Paula Cohen, *Signs* 1, no. 4 (1976): 879–80.

4. Louise Bogan, "American Literature," in *A Poet's Alphabet,* p. 12.

5. Freud, "Repression," p. 149.

6. Louise Bogan, "Hidden," *New Yorker* 11 (15 Feb. 1936): 20.

7. Elder Olson, "Louise Bogan and Léonie Adams," *Chicago Review* 8 (Fall 1954): 70. Reprinted in Collins, *Critical Essays on Louise Bogan,* p. 74.

8. Charles O. Hartmann, *Free Verse: An Essay on Prosody* (Princeton: Princeton University Press, 1980), p. 63.

9. Sandra M. Gilbert and Susan Gubar, *The Madwoman in the Attic: The Woman Writer and the Nineteenth-Century Literary Imagination* (New Haven: Yale University Press, 1984), 84.

10. Louise Bogan, "Detective Novels," in *A Poet's Alphabet,* p. 84.

11. Bogan to John Hall Wheelock, 13 Nov. 1929, in *What the Woman Lived,* p. 50.

12. Bogan, "Detective Novels," p. 86.

13. Ibid., p. 87.

14. Zabel, "Flower of the Mind," 162. Reprinted in Collins, *Critical Essays on Louise Bogan,* p. 36.

15. Yvor Winters, "The Poetry of Louise Bogan," *New Yorker,* 16 Oct. 1929, 247. Reprinted in Collins, *Critical Essays on Louise Bogan,* pp. 33–34.

16. Bogan to Wheelock, 12 Oct. 1929, in *What the Woman Lived,* pp. 48.

17. Marianne Moore, "Compactness Compacted," in *Predilections* (New York: Viking, 1955), p.130. Reprinted in Collins, *Critical Essays on Louise Bogan,* p. 61.

18. Ridgeway, *Louise Bogan,* p. 52.

19. Bowles, *Louise Bogan's Aesthetic of Limitation,* p. 98.

20. Paul Ramsey, "Louise Bogan," *Iowa Review* 1 (Summer 1970): 116. Reprinted in Collins, *Critical Essays on Louise Bogan,* p. 119.

21. Julia Kristeva, *Black Sun: Depression and Melancholia,* trans. Leon S. Roudiez (New York: Columbia University Press, 1989), p. 4.

22. Ibid., p. 42.

23. Frank, *Louise Bogan,* p. 51.

24. Ibid., p. 117.

25. Quoted in Ruth Lisa Schechter, "Louise Bogan: A Reminiscence," *Croton Review* 10 (1987): 33.

26. Bogan to Robert Phelps, 24 April 1957, in *What the Woman Lived,* p. 309.

27. Jacques Lacan, *The Four Fundamental Concepts of Psycho-Analysis,* ed. Jacques-Alain Miller, trans. Alan Sheridan (New York: Norton, 1981), p. 30.

28. Ibid., p. 43.

29. Allan Gardner Lloyd-Smith, *Uncanny American Fiction: Medusa's Face* (New York: St. Martin's, 1984), p. ix.

30. Bogan, "Heart and the Lyre," p. 429.

31. Bogan to Rufina McCarthy Helmer, 27 Feb. 1952, in *What the Woman Lived,* p. 277.

32. Sigmund Freud, "Mourning and Melancholia," in *The Standard Edition of the Complete Psychological Works of Sigmund Freud*, 14:244–45.

33. Bogan to Sarton, 17 March 1955, in *What the Woman Lived*, p. 295.

34. Bogan to Wheelock, 1 May 1929, in *What the Woman Lived*, p. 46.

35. Harold Bloom, "Louise Bogan Reads From Her Own Works," Yale Series of Recorded Poets, Decca Records, DL 9132. Reprinted in Collins, *Critical Essays on Louise Bogan*, pp. 84–85.

36. Cheryl Walker, *Masks Outrageous and Austere: Culture, Psyche, and Persona in Modern Women Poets* (Bloomington: Indiana University Press, 1991), p. 181.

37. Shoshana Felman, *Writing and Madness*, trans. Martha Noel Evans and the author with the assistance of Brian Massumi (Ithaca: Cornell University Press, 1985), p. 254.

38. W. H. Auden, "The Rewards of Patience," *Partisan Review* 9 (July–August 1942): 337. Reprinted in Collins, *Critical Essays on Louise Bogan*, p. 55.

Chapter 3. Recognition of the Maternal: *The Sleeping Fury*

1. Louise Bogan, "The Springs of Poetry," *New Republic* 37 (5 December 1923): 9.

2. Bogan to Harriet Monroe, 6 January 1930, in *What the Woman Lived*, p. 55.

3. Bogan to Wheelock, 11 April 1931, in *What the Woman Lived*, p. 57.

4. Bogan to Harriet Monroe, 23 June 1931, in *What the Woman Lived*, p. 59.

5. See Bogan to Sarton, 28 Jan. 1954, in *What the Woman Lived*, p. 282:

[W]hat has never been explained thoroughly, by me to you, is the really dreadful emotional state I was trapped in for many years—a state which Raymond struggled manfully against, I will say, for a long time. In those days, my devotion came out all counter-clockwise, as it were. I was a *demon* of jealousy, for example; and a sort of *demon* of fidelity, too: "morbid fidelity," Dr. Wall came to call it. A slave-maker, really, while remaining a sort of slave. Dreadful! Thank God v. little of it got into the poems; but the general warp showed up in every detail of my life.

6. Bogan to Wheelock, (June) 1936, in *What the Woman Lived*, p. 132.

7. Bogan to Roethke, 23 Aug. 1935, in *What the Woman Lived*, p. 96.

8. Louise Bogan, "Rainer Maria Rilke," in *A Poet's Alphabet*, p. 349.

9. Bogan to Zabel, 8 Dec. 1936, in *What the Woman Lived*, p. 145.

10. See Margaret Homans, *Bearing the Word: Language and Female Experience in Nineteenth-Century Women's Writing* (Chicago: University of Chicago Press, 1986), pp. 4–7.

11. Nancy Chodorow, *The Reproduction of Mothering: Psychoanalysis and the Sociology of Gender* (Berkeley: University of California Press, 1978), p. 110.

12. Homans, *Bearing the Word*, p. 14.

13. Julia Kristeva, *Desire in Language: A Semiotic Approach to Literature and Art*, ed. Leon S. Roudiez, trans. Thomas Gora, Alice Jardine, and Leon S. Roudiez (New York: Columbia University Press, 1980), p. 239.

14. Ibid., p. 133.

15. Ibid., p. 134.

16. Ibid., p. 138.

17. Homans, *Bearing the Word*, p. 25.

18. Ibid., p. 30.

19. Frank, *Louise Bogan*, pp. 4–5.

20. "A Night in Summer," in Louise Bogan Papers (Box 11, Folder 45), Special Collections Department, Amherst College Library. Noted by Elizabeth Frank as printed in 1911–12 *Jabberwock* and in the *Boston Evening Transcript*. See Frank, *Louise Bogan*, p. 28.

21. Frank, *Louise Bogan*, p. 10.

22. Josephine Donovan, *After the Fall: The Demeter-Persephone Myth in Wharton, Cather, and Glasgow* (University Park: Pennsylvania State University Press, 1989), pp. 165–66.

23. Bogan, "Situation in American Writing," p. 107. Reprinted in Collins, *Critical Essays on Louise Bogan*, p. 52.

24. Bogan to Allen Tate, 4 March 1941, in *What the Woman Lived*, p. 34n.

25. Bogan to Edmund Wilson (22 March 1939), in *What the Woman Lived*, p. 185.

26. John Muller, "Light and the Wisdom of the Dark: Aging and the Language of Desire in the Texts of Louise Bogan," in *Memory and Desire: Aging-Literature-Psychoanalysis*, ed. Kathleen Woodward and Murry S. Schwartz (Bloomington: Indiana University Press, 1986), p. 77.

27. Ibid., p. 80.

28. Ibid., p. 87.

29. Louise Bogan, "Art Embroidery," *New Republic* 54 (21 March 1928): 156.

30. Bogan, "Heart and the Lyre," pp. 427–28.

31. Roethke, "Poetry of Louise Bogan," p. 138.

32. Karen Elias-Button, "The Muse as Medusa," in *The Lost Tradition: Mothers and Daughters in Literature*, ed. Cathy N. Davidson and E. M. Broner (New York: Frederick Ungar, 1980), p. 205.

33. As Deborah Pope points out, "The male-female tension is emphasized in the third stanza by two patently phallic images and two female images—'Rocket and tree, and dome and bubble'—which are, to the speaker, images of treachery." *A Separate Vision*, p. 37.

34. See Ruth Limmer's note on Coffey in Bogan, *What the Woman Lived*, p. 3: "John Coffey [was] a young Irishman who, so he claimed, thought to call attention to the needs of the poor by shoplifting (his specialty was furs) and then, in court, with attendant publicity, testifying to their plight. The plan went awry: having told the police of his long-term, successful thefts, he was sent not to court but to Matteawan, an insane asylum."

35. In Louise Bogan Papers (Box 20, Folder 4), Special Collections Department, Amherst College Library. The quotation is from Otto Fenichel's *Outline of Clinical Psychoanalysis*, trans. Bertram D. Lewin and Gregory Zilboorg (New York: Psychoanalytic Quarterly Press & Norton, 1934), p. 392.

36. Fenichel, *Outline of Clinical Psychoanalysis*, pp. 392–93.

37. Bogan to Sister M. Angela, 20 Aug. 1966, in *What the Woman Lived*, p. 368.

38. Bogan to Wilson, 2 May 1931, in *What the Woman Lived*, p. 58.

39. Bogan to Harriet Monroe, 23 June 1931, in *What the Woman Lived*, p. 59.

40. Bogan to Zabel, 19 Jan. 1939, in *What the Woman Lived*, pp. 181–82.

41. Bogan to Humphries, 17 March 1939, in *What the Woman Lived*, p. 184.

42. Bogan to Wheelock, (June) 1936, in *What the Woman Lived*, p. 132.

43. Kenneth Rexroth, "Louise Bogan's Verse Adjusted to Wisdom and Mellow Style," review of *The Sleeping Fury*, by Louise Bogan, *San Francisco Chronicle*, 25 July 1937, column 1, 4D. Reprinted in Collins, *Critical Essays on Louise Bogan*, p. 40.

44. Ibid., column 2, 4D. Reprinted in Collins, *Critical Essays on Louise Bogan*, p. 41.

45. Allen Tate, review of *The Sleeping Fury*, by Louise Bogan, *Southern Review* 3 (Summer 1937): 190–91. Reprinted in Collins, *Critical Essays on Louise Bogan* p. 41.

46. Ford Madox Ford, "The Flame in Stone," *Poetry* 50 (June 1937): 158. Reprinted in Collins, *Critical Essays on Louise Bogan*, p. 46.

47. Bogan to Sarton, 21 April 1954, in *What the Woman Lived*, p. 286.

48. "The Sleeping Fury," in Louise Bogan Papers (Box 11, Folder 62), Special Collections Department, Amherst College Library.

49. "The Lie," in Louise Bogan Papers (Box 11, Folder 33), Special Collections Department, Amherst College Library.

50. Bogan to Zabel, 23 Dec. 1936, in *What the Woman Lived*, p. 147.

51. Bogan to Zabel, 27 Dec. 1936, in *What the Woman Lived*, p. 147.

52. Frank, *Louise Bogan,* p. 263.

53. Ridgeway, *Louise Bogan,* p. 93.

54. In Louise Bogan Papers (Box 11, Folder 35), Special Collections Department, Amherst College Library.

55. Bogan to Rufina McCarthy Helmer, 25 July 1966, in *What the Woman Lived*, p. 368.

56. Lawrence Lipking, *Abandoned Women and Poetic Tradition* (Chicago: University of Chicago Press, 1988), p. 25.

57. Bogan to Zabel, 10 Aug. 1936, in *What the Woman Lived*, p. 136.

Chapter 4. Imagining Release: The Later Poems

1. Bogan to Zabel, 27 July 1934, in *What the Woman Lived*, p. 79.

2. Ruth Limmer, "Circumscriptions," in Collins, *Critical Essays on Louise Bogan*, p. 172.

3. Tillie Olsen, *Silences* (New York: Delacorte, 1978), p. 145.

4. Bowles, *Louise Bogan's Aesthetics of Limitation,* p. 1. Marcia Aldrich pursues this line of reasoning further, linking Bogan's small late output of poetry to negative conceptions of menopause: "Having defined her inspiration as romantic love, an eroticism of physical sensation depending on male dominance and female abasement, Bogan found she could no longer fulfill that role [in midlife]." "Lethal Brevity: Louise Bogan's Lyric Career," in *Aging and Literature: Studies in Creativity,* ed. Anne M. Wyatt-Brown and Janice Rossen (Charlottesville: University Press of Virginia, 1993), p. 116.

I would argue that Bogan's declared focus on maturity and her early subversive critiques of romantic love render her responses to aging as inevitably more complex than Aldrich's argument allows. To defend her argument, Aldrich must disallow, unfortunately, much of Bogan's own work as a self-reflective critic, writing in her first endnote that "Bogan's criticism is often of little use—sometimes even deceptive—in reading her poetry" (p. 120).

5. I am indebted to Jeredith Merrin for this suggestion.

6. Bogan to John Hall Wheelock, (June) 1936, in *What the Woman Lived*, pp. 132–33.

7. Bogan, "Springs of Poetry," p. 9.

8. A. Donald Douglas, review of *Body of This Death*, by Louise Bogan, *New Republic* 37 (5 Dec. 1923): 20.

9. Bogan to Zabel, 10 Aug. 1936, in *What the Woman Lived*, p. 135.

10. Bogan to Sarton, 28 Jan. 1954, in *What the Woman Lived*, p. 283.

11. Bogan to Sarton, 6 Sept. 1962, in *What the Woman Lived*, p. 347.

12. DeShazer, *Inspiring Women*, p. 61.

13. Ibid., p. 57.

14. Bogan to Sarton, 13 Nov. 1959, in *What the Woman Lived*, p. 317.

15. Louise Bogan, "Paul Eluard," in *A Poet's Alphabet*, p. 115.

16. Louise Bogan, "Anthologies," in *A Poet's Alphabet*, p. 29.

17. Louise Bogan, "Muriel Rukeyser (1939)," in *A Poet's Alphabet*, p. 229.

18. Bogan, "Paul Eluard," in *A Poet's Alphabet*, p. 115.

19. Ibid., p. 113.

20. Ibid., p. 115.

21. Ibid., p. 116.

22. Louise Bogan, "Mythologies," in *A Poet's Alphabet*, p. 311.

23. Ibid., p. 312.

24. Bogan, "Emily Dickinson," in *A Poet's Alphabet*, p. 96

25. Bogan, in Paul Engle and Joseph Langland, eds., *Poet's Choice* (New York: Dial, 1962), pp. 33–34.

26. Ibid., p. 34.

27. Bogan to Sarton, 14 Aug. 1954, in *What the Woman Lived*, p. 369n.

28. Bogan to Sister M. Angela, 20 Aug. 1966, in *What the Woman Lived*, p. 368.

29. Marianne Moore, "Compactness Compacted," p. 130. Reprinted in Collins, *Critical Essays on Louise Bogan*, p. 61.

30. W. H. Auden, "The Rewards of Patience," *Partisan Review* 9 (1942): 339. Reprinted in Collins, *Critical Essays on Louise Bogan*, p. 57.

31. Malcolm Cowley, "Three Poets," *New Republic,* 10 November 1941, p. 625. Reprinted in Collins, *Critical Essays on Louise Bogan*, p. 58.

32. Stanley Kunitz, "Land of Dust and Flame," in *A Kind of Order, A Kind of Folly* (Boston: Little, Brown, 1975), p. 197. Reprinted in Collins, *Critical Essays on Louise Bogan*, p. 64.

33. Louise Bogan, "Edna Millay (1939)," in *A Poet's Alphabet*, p. 299.

34. Bogan to Roethke, 23 August 1935, in *What the Woman Lived*, p. 97.

35. Bogan to Zabel, 20 March 1948, in *What the Woman Lived*, p. 261.

36. Bogan to Roethke, (Sept.) 1937, in *What the Woman Lived*, p. 163.

37. See Frank, *Louise Bogan*, p. 359.

38. Bogan to Sarton, 4 Feb. 1954, in *What the Woman Lived*, pp. 283–84.

39. In Louise Bogan Papers (Box 20, Folder 4), Special Collections Department, Amherst College Library.

40. Louise Bogan, "The Collected Poetry of W. H. Auden," in *A Poet's Alphabet*, p. 40.

41. Bogan to Zabel, 5 Feb. 1935, in *What the Woman Lived*, p. 83–84.

42. "Letter to Mrs. Q's Sister," in Louise Bogan Papers (Box 11, Folder 43), Special Collections Department, Amherst College Library.

43. See May Sarton, *A World of Light: Portraits and Celebrations* (New York: Norton, 1976), p. 229: "The poem reads like the culmination of a long passionate love affair, but was actually inspired by Louise having sat next to T. S. Eliot at a dinner party!"

44. Bogan to Humphries, Jan. 1949, in *What the Woman Lived*, p. 267n.

45. Marianne Moore, "Compactness Compacted," p. 133. Reprinted in Collins, *Critical Essays on Louise Bogan*, p. 63.

46. Bogan, "Emily Dickinson," in *A Poet's Alphabet*, p. 102.

47. William Meredith, "Poems of a Human Being," *New York Times Book Review,* 13 Oct. 1968, p. 4. Reprinted in Collins, *Critical Essays on Louise Bogan*, p. 97.

48. William Heyen, "The Distance from our Eyes," *Prairie Schooner* 43 (Fall 1969): 326. Reprinted in Collins, *Critical Essays on Louise Bogan*, p. 101.

49. Bogan to Wheelock, 16 Feb. 1956, in *What the Woman Lived*, p. 308.

50. Bogan to Glenway Wescott, 15 March 1957, in *What the Woman Lived*, p. 309n.

51. Bogan to Sarton (4 Feb. 1954), in *What the Woman Lived*, p. 283.

52. Bogan, in *What the Woman Lived*, Limmer's note, p. 372n.

53. Bogan to Howard Moss, 25 Jan. 1967, in *What the Woman Lived*, p. 371.

54. Limmer, "Circumscriptions," p. 174.

55. See Bowles, *Louise Bogan's Aesthetic of Limitation,* p. 137: "[T]he poet was valiantly fighting off the effects of Librium, which gave her brief relief from depression and then brought on fits of weeping."

56. Auden, "The Rewards of Patience," p. 337. Reprinted in Collins, *Critical Essays on Louise Bogan*, p. 55.

57. René Girard, *Violence and the Sacred*, trans. Patrick Gregory (Baltimore: Johns Hopkins University Press, 1977), p. 168.

58. Walker, *Nightingale's Burden*, p. 149.

59. Bogan to Limmer, 23 Feb. 1969, in *What the Woman Lived*, p. 377.

60. Bogan to Limmer, 10 March 1969, in *What the Woman Lived*, p. 378.

61. Bogan, *Selected Criticism: Poetry and Prose* (New York: Noonday, 1955), p. 5.

Works Cited

Adams, Léonie. "All Has Been Translated into Treasure." *Poetry* 85 (December 1954): 165–69.

Aldrich, Marcia. "Lethal Brevity: Louise Bogan's Lyric Career." In *Aging and Gender in Literature: Studies in Creativity,* edited by Anne M. Wyatt-Brown and Janice Rossen, pp. 105–20. Charlottesville: University Press of Virginia, 1993.

Auden, W. H. "The Rewards of Patience." *Partisan Review* 9 (1942): 336–40.

Bennett, Paula. *My Life a Loaded Gun: Female Creativity and Feminist Poetics.* Boston: Beacon, 1986.

Bloom, Harold. "Louise Bogan Reads From Her Own Works." Yale Series of Recorded Poets, Decca Records, DL 9132.

Bogan, Louise. *Achievement in American Poetry.* Chicago: Henry Regnery, 1951.

———. "Art Embroidery." *New Republic* 54 (21 March 1928): 156.

———. *The Blue Estuaries: Poems, 1923–1968.* New York: Ecco, 1977.

———. *Body of This Death.* New York: Robert M. McBride, 1923.

———. *Journey Around My Room: The Autobiography of Louise Bogan, A Mosaic.* Edited by Ruth Limmer. New York: Viking, 1980.

———. "Poetesses in the Parlor." *New Yorker* 12 (5 Dec. 1936): 42, 45–56, 48, 50, 52.

———. *A Poet's Alphabet.* Edited by Robert Phelps and Ruth Limmer. New York: McGraw-Hill, 1970.

———. *Selected Criticism: Poetry and Prose.* New York: Noonday, 1955.

———. "The Situation in American Writing: Seven Questions." *Partisan Review* 6 (Fall 1939): 105–8.

———. "The Springs of Poetry." *New Republic* 37 (5 December 1923): 9.

———. "Virginia Woolf on Women." Review of *A Room of One's Own,* by Virginia Woolf. *New Republic* 61 (18 December 1929): 105.

———. *What the Woman Lived: Selected Letters of Louise Bogan, 1920–1970.* Edited by Ruth Limmer. New York: Harcourt Brace Jovanovich, 1973.

Bowles, Gloria. *Louise Bogan's Aesthetic of Limitation.* Bloomington: Indiana University Press, 1987.

Chodorow, Nancy. *The Reproduction of Mothering: Psychoanalysis and the Sociology of Gender*. Berkeley: University of California Press, 1978.

Cixous, Hélène. "The Laugh of the Medusa." Translated by Keith Cohen and Paula Cohen. *Signs* 1, no. 4 (1976): 875–93.

Clark, Suzanne. *Sentimental Modernism: Women Writers and the Revolution of the Word*. Bloomington: Indiana University Press, 1991.

Collins, Martha, ed. *Critical Essays on Louise Bogan*. Boston: G. K. Hall, 1984.

Cowley, Malcolm. "Three Poets." *New Republic* 105 (10 November 1941): 625–26.

Daniels, Kate. "The Demise of the 'Delicate Prisons': The Women's Movement in Twentieth-Century American Poetry." In *A Profile of Twentieth-Century American Poetry*, edited by Jack Myers and David Wojahn, pp. 224–53. Carbondale: Southern Illinois University Press, 1991.

DeShazer, Mary K. *Inspiring Women: Reimagining the Muse*. New York: Holmes and Meier, 1980.

Deutsch, Babette. *Poetry in Our Time*. New York: Columbia University Press, 1956.

Dodd, Elizabeth. *The Veiled Mirror and the Woman Poet: H.D., Louise Bogan, Elizabeth Bishop, and Louise Glück*. Columbia: University of Missouri Press, 1992.

Donovan, Josephine. *After the Fall: The Demeter-Persephone Myth in Wharton, Cather, and Glasgow*. University Park: Pennsylvania State University Press, 1989.

Douglas, Donald A. Review of *Body of This Death*, by Louise Bogan. *New Republic* 37 (5 December 1923): 20, 22.

Elias-Button, Karen. "The Muse as Medusa." In *The Lost Tradition: Mothers and Daughters in Literature*, edited by Cathy N. Davidson and E. M. Broner, pp. 193–206. New York: Frederick Ungar, 1980.

Engle, Paul, and Joseph Langland, eds. *Poet's Choice*. New York: Dial, 1962.

Felman, Shoshana. *Writing and Madness*. Translated by Martha Noel Evans and the author with the assistance of Brian Massumi. Ithaca: Cornell University Press, 1985.

Fenichel, Otto. *Outline of Clinical Psychoanalysis*. Translated by Bertram D. Lewin and Gregory Zilboorg. New York: Psychoanalytic Quarterly Press & Norton, 1934.

Ford, Ford Madox. "The Flame in the Stone." *Poetry* 50 (June 1937): 158–61.

Frank, Elizabeth. *Louise Bogan: A Portrait*. New York: Knopf, 1985.

Freud, Sigmund. "Mourning and Melancholia." In *The Standard Edition of the Complete Psychological Works of Sigmund Freud*, translated by James Strachey, 14:243–58. London: Hogarth, 1978.

———. "Repression." In *The Standard Edition of the Complete Psychological Works of Sigmund Freud*, translated by James Strachey, 14:146–58. London: Hogarth, 1978.

———. "The Unconscious." In *The Standard Edition of the Complete Psychological Works of Sigmund Freud*, translated by James Strachey, 14:166–204. London: Hogarth, 1978.

Gilbert, Sandra M., and Susan Gubar. *The Madwoman in the Attic: The Woman Writer and the Nineteenth-Century Literary Imagination*. New Haven: Yale University Press, 1984.

———, eds. *Shakespeare's Sisters: Feminist Essays on Women Poets*. Bloomington: Indiana University Press, 1979.

Giles, Ronald. "The Ironic Voice in Louise Bogan's 'Women'." *Poesis: A Journal of Criticism* 7, no. 5 (1987): 34–41.

Girard, René. *Violence and the Sacred.* Translated by Patrick Gregory. Baltimore: Johns Hopkins University Press, 1977.

Hartmann, Charles O. *Free Verse: An Essay on Prosody.* Princeton: Princeton University Press, 1980.

Heyen, William. "The Distance From Our Eyes." Review of *The Blue Estuaries,* by Louise Bogan. *Prairie Schooner* 43 (Fall 1969): 323–26.

Homans, Margaret. *Bearing the Word: Language and Female Experience in Nineteenth-Century Women's Writing.* Chicago: University of Chicago Press, 1986.

Jones, Llewellyn. *First Impressions: Essays on Poetry, Criticism, and Prosody.* 1925. Reprint, Freeport, N.Y.: Books for Libraries Press.

Kristeva, Julia. *Black Sun: Depression and Melancholia.* Translated by Leon S. Roudiez. New York: Columbia University Press, 1989.

———. *Desire in Language: A Semiotic Approach to Literature and Art.* Edited by Leon S. Roudiez. Translated by Thomas Gora, Alice Jardine, and Leon S. Roudiez. New York: Columbia University Press, 1980.

———. *Revolution in Poetic Language.* Translated by Margaret Waller. New York: Columbia University Press, 1984.

Kunitz, Stanley. *A Kind of Order, A Kind of Folly: Essays and Conversations.* Boston: Little, Brown, 1975.

Lacan, Jacques. *The Four Fundamental Concepts of Psycho-Analysis.* Edited by Jacques-Alain Miller. Translated by Alan Sheridan. New York: Norton, 1981.

Larsen, Jeanne. "Lowell, Teasdale, Wylie, Millay, and Bogan." In *The Columbia History of American Poetry*, edited by Jay Parini and Brett C. Millie, pp. 203–32. New York: Columbia University Press, 1993.

Lechlitner, Ruth. "Mistress of Poetic Forms." *New York Herald Tribune Review of Books,* 30 May 1937, 2.

Limmer, Ruth. "Circumscriptions." In *Critical Essays on Louise Bogan*, edited by Martha Collins, pp. 166–74. Boston: G. K. Hall, 1984.

Lipking, Lawrence. *Abandoned Women and Poetic Tradition.* Chicago: University of Chicago Press, 1988.

Lloyd-Smith, Allan Gardner. *Uncanny American Fiction: Medusa's Face.* New York: St. Martin's, 1984.

Meredith, William. *New York Times Book Review*, 13 October 1968, 4.

Moldaw, Carol. "Form, Feeling, and Nature: Aspects of Harmony in the Poetry of Louise Bogan." In *Critical Essays on Louise Bogan*, edited by Martha Collins, pp. 180–94. Boston: G. K. Hall, 1984.

Moore, Marianne. "Compactness Compacted." In *Predilections*, pp. 130–33. New York: Viking, 1955.

Moore, Patrick. "Symbol, Mask, and Meter in the Poetry of Louise Bogan." In *Gender and Literary Voice*, edited by Janet Todd, pp. 67–80. New York: Holmes and Meier, 1980.

Muller, John. "Light and the Wisdom of the Dark: Aging and the Language of Desire in the Texts of Louise Bogan." In *Memory and Desire: Aging-Literature-Psychoanalysis*, edited by Kathleen Woodward and Murray S. Schwartz, pp. 76–96. Bloomington: Indiana University Press, 1986.

Olsen, Tillie. *Silences*. New York: Delacorte, 1978.

Olson, Elder. "Louise Bogan and Léonie Adams." *Chicago Review* 8 (Fall 1954): 70–87.

Pais, Sara Via. "Shapes of the Feminine Experience in Art." In *Women, the Arts, and the 1920s in Paris and New York*, edited by Kenneth W. Wheeler and Virginia Lee Lussier, pp. 49–55. New Brunswick, N.J.: Transaction Books, 1982.

Pope, Deborah. "Music in the Granite Hill: The Poetry of Louise Bogan." In *Critical Essays on Louise Bogan*, edited by Martha Collins, pp. 149–66. Boston: G. K. Hall, 1984.

———. *A Separate Vision: Isolation in Contemporary Women's Poetry*. Baton Rouge: Louisiana State University Press, 1984.

Ramsey, Paul. "Louise Bogan." *The Iowa Review* 1 (Summer 1970): 116–24.

Rexroth, Kenneth. Foreword to *The Poetic Vision of Muriel Rukeyser*, by Louise Kertesz, pp. xi–xvi. Baton Rouge: Louisiana State University Press, 1980.

———. "Louise Bogan's Verse Adjusted to Wisdom and Mellow Style." Review of *The Sleeping Fury*, by Louise Bogan. *San Francisco Chronicle*, 25 July 1937, p. 4D.

Ridgeway, Jaqueline. *Louise Bogan*. Boston: Twayne, 1984.

Roethke, Theodore. "The Poetry of Louise Bogan." In *The Poet and His Craft: Selected Prose of Theodore Roethke*, edited by Ralph J. Mills Jr., pp. 133–48. Seattle: University of Washington Press, 1965.

Sarton, May. *A World of Light: Portraits and Celebrations*. New York: Norton, 1976.

Schechter, Ruth Lisa. "Louise Bogan: A Reminiscence." *Croton Review* 10 (1987): 30–33.

Sell, Gwendolyn Sorrell. "Louise Bogan: The Discipline of Recognition: Gender and Artistic Maturity." Diss., Emory University, 1988.

Tate, Allen. "R. P. Blackmur and Others." *Southern Review* 3 (1937): 183–98.

Untermeyer, Louis. "In a Gold Stain." *Saturday Review*, 1 February 1930, 692.

Van Doren, Mark. "Louise Bogan." *Nation*, 31 October 1923, 494.

Walker, Cheryl. *Masks Outrageous and Austere: Culture, Psyche, and Persona in Modern Women Poets*. Bloomington: Indiana University Press, 1991.

———. *The Nightingale's Burden: Women Poets and Culture Before 1900*. Bloomington: Indiana University Press, 1982.

Winters, Yvor. "The Poetry of Louise Bogan." *New Republic* 60 (16 October 1929): 247–48.

Zabel, Morton D. "The Flower of the Mind." *Poetry* 35 (December 1929): 158–62.

Index

167